Contents

Introduction

WORKING LIFE is Volume 335 in the **ISSUES** series. The aim of the series is to offer current, diverse information about important issues in our world, from a UK perspective.

ABOUT WORKING LIFE

Youth unemployment is currently at one of the lowest levels that it has been for a decade. However, it is still an issue for many young people who are looking for employment. This book explores employment in the UK and the issues faced by young people looking for employment such as routes into work, benefits available and employment statuses.

OUR SOURCES

Titles in the **ISSUES** series are designed to function as educational resource books, providing a balanced overview of a specific subject.

The information in our books is comprised of facts, articles and opinions from many different sources, including:

⇨ Newspaper reports and opinion pieces

⇨ Website factsheets

⇨ Magazine and journal articles

⇨ Statistics and surveys

⇨ Government reports

⇨ Literature from special interest groups.

A NOTE ON CRITICAL EVALUATION

Because the information reprinted here is from a number of different sources, readers should bear in mind the origin of the text and whether the source is likely to have a particular bias when presenting information (or when conducting their research). It is hoped that, as you read about the many aspects of the issues explored in this book, you will critically evaluate the information presented.

It is important that you decide whether you are being presented with facts or opinions. Does the writer give a biased or unbiased report? If an opinion is being expressed, do you agree with the writer? Is there potential bias to the 'facts' or statistics behind an article?

ASSIGNMENTS

In the back of this book, you will find a selection of assignments designed to help you engage with the articles you have been reading and to explore your own opinions. Some tasks will take longer than others and there is a mixture of design, writing and research-based activities that you can complete alone or in a group.

Useful weblinks

www.aat.org.uk

www.acas.org.uk

www.bupa.co.uk

www.economicsonline.co.uk

www.fullfact.org

www.gov.uk

www.huffingtonpost.co.uk

www.impetus-pef.org.uk

www.independent.co.uk

www.jrf.org.uk

www.le.ac.uk

www.ons.gov.uk

www.prospects.ac.uk

www.replgroup.com

www.successatschool.org

www.telegraph.co.uk

www.theconversation.com

www.theweek.co.uk

www.ucl.ac.uk

www.wearerestless.org

www.ymca.org.uk

FURTHER RESEARCH

At the end of each article we have listed its source and a website that you can visit if you would like to conduct your own research. Please remember to critically evaluate any sources that you consult and consider whether the information you are viewing is accurate and unbiased.

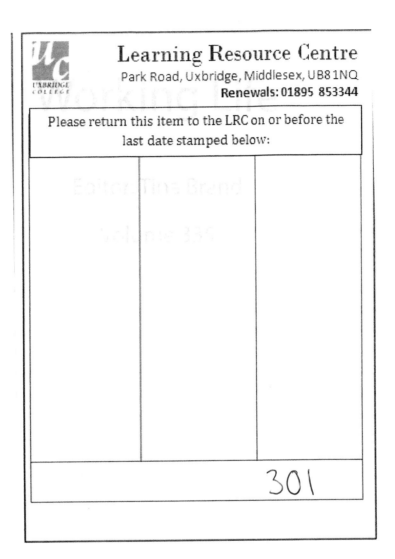

Independence Educational Publishers

First published by Independence Educational Publishers

The Studio, High Green

Great Shelford

Cambridge CB22 5EG

England

ISBN-13: 978 1 86168 786 9

Printed in Great Britain

Zenith Print Group

What is unemployment?

What is unemployment?

To be classed as unemployed you have to be out of work and actively seeking work.

If you are not in work and don't want to be in work, maybe because you are retired or because you are looking after a child or loved one, you don't count as unemployed.

The official definition of 'unemployed' is someone who is not in work, has looked for work in the last four weeks and is ready to start work in the next two weeks. It also includes people who are out of work, but have found a job and are waiting to start it in the next two weeks.

How is unemployment measured in the UK?

Unemployment is measured by a survey of 100,000 adults aged 16 and over in 40,000 households in the UK. The survey uses a random sample of addresses.

The Office for National Statistics (ONS) then uses the survey results to estimate the total number of people who are unemployed across the UK.

This is separate to the claimant count which measures the number of people claiming benefits because they are out of work. It includes people who are on Jobseeker's Allowance and people claiming Universal Credit, where claimants have to be seeking work to qualify.

How many people are unemployed in the UK?

1.4 million adults were unemployed in the UK between August and October 2017 (the latest figure).

The UK claimant count was 817,000 in November 2017. This is much lower than the number of unemployed people because the claimant count does not specifically measure unemployment. It excludes people who do not claim unemployment benefits, even if they are looking for work. It may also include a small number of people who are actually in work: for example, people who may work a very small number of hours on a low wage and who are seeking full-time work and so qualify for unemployment benefits.

What is the unemployment rate?

The unemployment rate is the number of unemployed people as a percentage of all 'economically active' people. 'Economically active' is statistical speak for people who are either in work or who want to be.

It counts people who are employed plus those who are unemployed and looking for work. The rate is calculated this way because statisticians are trying to count how many people who want a job don't have one, not just how many people are not in work.

4.3% of people aged 16 and over were unemployed from August to October 2017 – that's around one in every 23 people who want to work. This is down from 4.8% a year earlier and the lowest it has been since 1975.

What is the youth unemployment rate?

This is the unemployment rate specifically for people aged 16 to 24. It includes people who are looking for work and people who are still in full-time education looking for a part-time job. The ONS says "it is a common misconception that all people in full-time education are classified as economically inactive."

523,000 young people were unemployed from August to October 2017 (including 186,000 full-time students looking for part-time work).

This means the unemployment rate for 16- to 24-year-olds was 12%. This figure is lower than at the same time a year earlier (13%) and is the lowest it has been since 2004.

What is structural unemployment?

Structural unemployment is unemployment based on significant changes to the environment businesses work in – for example a change in technology, or government policy – rather than just the ups and downs of the economy.

For example it could be caused by technology changing more quickly than people can learn the skills they need for new industries. As a result, some people become unemployed or struggle to find work because fewer jobs require the skills they have. For example, think of how quickly personal computers have made typewriting jobs redundant.

What is cyclical unemployment?

Cyclical unemployment is related to the health of the economy. When the economy is not doing well businesses lose money and lay off people to try and reduce their costs. And so unemployment goes up.

When the economy recovers businesses hire more people to keep up with increased demand for their products and services. And so unemployment goes down.

13 December 2017

⇨ The above information is reprinted with kind permission from Full Fact. Please visit www.fullfact.org for further information.

Employment status

A number of different working arrangements have developed over the years, allowing more flexibility at work. There are three main types of employment status.

⇨ Employee

⇨ Worker

⇨ Self-employed.

An individual's employment rights will depend upon whether they are an employee or worker (the self-employed have very few employment rights).

Key points

⇨ Employees have more employment rights than workers, so if a right applies to a worker it also applies to an employee.

⇨ Workers are entitled to certain employment rights such as the national minimum wage and paid annual leave.

⇨ Apprenticeships are work-based training programmes which lead to a nationally recognised qualification.

⇨ Volunteers carry out unpaid work for organisations such as charities or fund-raising organisations.

⇨ Students are often required to go through an internship as part of their education.

Employee

An employee will work to the terms within a contract of employment, and will carry out the work personally. A contract exists when terms such as pay, annual leave and working hours are agreed. Although the contract doesn't have to be written down to be valid it is best to record the main terms and conditions of employment in writing.

Employees are entitled to a wide range of employment rights, including all those to which a worker is entitled.

Examples of employee rights include:

⇨ written statement of employment

⇨ itemised pay slip

⇨ the National Minimum Wage

⇨ holiday pay, maternity and paternity pay, etc.

⇨ the right to request flexible working hours

⇨ the right not to be discriminated against.

Worker

A worker will also work to the terms within a contract of employment and generally have to carry out the work personally. However, some workers may have a limited right to send someone else to carry out the work, such as a sub-contractor.

Workers could include:

⇨ casual work

⇨ agency workers

⇨ freelance work

⇨ seasonal work

⇨ zero-hours work.

Workers are entitled to some employment rights including:

⇨ the National Minimum Wage

⇨ holiday pay

⇨ protection against unlawful discrimination

⇨ the right not to be treated less favourably if they work part-time.

Self-employed

A self-employed person will run their own business and take responsibility for the success of the business. Self-employed people are more likely to be contracted to provide a service for a client. They will not be paid through PAYE and don't have the same employment rights and responsibilities as employees or workers.

However, a self-employed person:

⇨ still has protection for their health and safety on a client's premises

⇨ in some cases will be protected against discrimination

⇨ will have their rights and responsibilities set out in the terms of the contract with their client

⇨ in general will not have right to holiday pay

⇨ may in limited cases be self-employed for tax purposes but classed as a worker or an employee for employment rights.

Agency workers

An agency worker is supplied by a temporary work agency to a client/hirer to carry out work for the client/hirer. The work is normally for a temporary period.

The Agency Workers Regulations give agency workers the right to the same basic working and employment conditions they would receive if directly engaged by the client to do the same job.

Apprentices

School leavers can still leave school at 16 in England and Wales but must continue their education until they are 18 which could include becoming an apprentice. School leavers in Scotland can still leave school without going into further training.

Apprenticeships are work-based training programmes which lead to

nationally recognised qualifications. Apprentices normally attend local colleges or specialist training providers on a day release basis as part of their training. Depending on the level, apprenticeships can take between one to four years to complete.

Apprentices under 19, or 19 years and over in the first year of their apprenticeship, are entitled to be paid the apprentice national minimum wage. However, employers can pay a higher rate if they choose to. Once an apprentice reaches 19 years and has completed the first year of the apprenticeship the employer must pay the full national minimum wage rate.

All other apprentices are entitled to the national minimum wage based on their age.

Interns

Intern's are graduates or students who spend a fixed amount of time working to gain skills and experience in a particular industry or sector. Students often have to do an internship as part of their further or higher education course.

An interns employment rights will depend on their employment status. If they are classed as a worker then they're normally entitled to the national minimum wage. However, if the internship is part of a UK-based further or higher education course (a sandwich course) lasting less than a year then interns are not normally entitled to the National Minimum Wage.

Internships should not be confused with work experience which involves a person spending a limited period with an employer to learn about working life and the working environment.

Volunteers

Volunteers carry out unpaid work for organisations such charities, voluntary organisations or fund-raising bodies. Volunteers usually have a volunteering agreement and a role description rather than a contract of employment and a job description. They should receive training and development appropriate to their role.

Volunteers are not entitled to the national minimum wage as they are not paid for their services, but they are often paid their travel and lunch expenses.

Umbrella companies

An umbrella company is a company that will act as an employer to agency contractors who work under a fixed term contract assignment. The umbrella company will normally sign a business-to-business contract with the recruitment agency, and the agency will sign a contract with the client. The agency will invoice the client for completed work, the client pays the agency, and the agency then pays the umbrella company. This money becomes the umbrella company's income. The umbrella company deducts the necessary tax and NI contributions, including employers NI, and any other deduction necessary, which means the payment will be made through PAYE.

⇨ The above information is reprinted with kind permission from ACAS. Please visit www.acas.org.uk for further information.

Young people are right to feel hard done by – pay discrimination for under-25s is legal

THE CONVERSATION

An article from **The Conversation.**

Sandhya Drew, Associate Tutor in Public, Employment and Equality Law, University of Surrey

Many of the university students graduating in the coming months are likely to feel short-changed when they start looking for jobs. Until they reach their 25th birthdays, and regardless of their qualifications, the minimum hourly rate they can be paid is £7.05 gross. That is 45p an hour less than the absolute minimum payable to someone 25 years old and over, for the same job. The rates are even lower for those under 21 and under 18.

This is because the law allows age discrimination in minimum wages – but only for the low-paid. The exemption doesn't apply if the person is earning over the National Living Wage (NLW) – introduced by the Conservatives in 2016. Yet, as of April 2017, 8.5% of the workforce is on one of the minimum rates.

A National Minimum Wage was introduced in 1998 by the Labour Government to fulfil a manifesto pledge to tackle low pay and poverty. From the outset, distinctions were made for rates for apprentices, but the adult rate applied to those over 21 and not in full-time education.

When, in the face of a mounting campaign for a higher living wage, the Conservative Government introduced the NLW in 2016, it decided to exclude under 25-year-olds and create a new age band for 21–24-year-olds. Those over 25 saw an increase of 4.3% in the minimum wage while under-25s saw 3.2%. The NLW is a commitment to phase in a significant wage increase for those above 25 with a target of £9 an hour by 2020.

Where the parties stand

Three of the main parties have picked up the issue in their election campaigning. The Labour Party manifesto promises to raise the minimum wage to the level of the NLW for all workers over 18. The Green Party will proceed by scrapping age-related wage bands and raising the national minimum wage to living wage levels for all. The Scottish National Party manifesto is the most far-reaching and supports the Real Living Wage of £8.45 for all adults over 18.

The Liberal Democrats' manifesto vows to promote the adoption of the living wage but is silent on the exclusion of under-25s from it. The Conservatives have pledged to increase the NLW to 60% of median earnings by 2020 and thereafter by the rate of median earnings – but there is no proposal to include under-25s. The UKIP manifesto says it will enforce the living and national wages and increase the number of minimum wage inspectors. It says nothing about the under-25 exclusion.

Is the discrimination justified?

Although it has not yet faced a legal challenge, the under-25 exclusion could yet be challenged in court for unjustified age discrimination. An EU equality directive on this issue is still applicable while the UK remains part of the EU. It allows countries to legislate for age discrimination, but only where the discrimination fulfils a legitimate aim. Justification of discrimination must be specific and based on evidence.

In his July 2015 budget speech, the then-chancellor, George Osborne, gave no reason for the NLW applying only to working people over 25. A government evidence document published that autumn was more specific and justified excluding workers under 25 "in order to maximise the opportunities for younger workers to gain … experience".

The Government receives annual advice about pay from the Low Pay Commission which considers evidence from the labour market. In its autumn 2016 report, the commission found that the NLW had started to have an

inflationary effect on median pay but that this effect was less pronounced for the under-25s. While noting an increase in employment for the 21 to 25 age group, it said that more younger workers were being hired. It didn't explicitly say so, but it's possible that this is because they were cheaper for employers to hire.

Since the Brexit vote, there are already reports of fewer takers for low-pay jobs that had previously been sought by young EU citizens. If this continues, it's possible that a less crowded labour market may actually remove one of the arguments in favour of a lower minimum rate – because there will be fewer young workers competing for jobs, though this would depend in turn on the state of the economy.

Labour-market policy generally, and justifications for discrimination specifically, must be constantly reviewed in light of changing social conditions. The exclusion does not look cogent and the evidence underpinning it could well change. In Europe, only Greece and the UK draw the line at 25.

Since the election was called, 1.05 million 18- to 24-year-olds have registered to vote. Equal access to the NLW for those among them in low pay or risking it may not be the only issue they consider at the ballot box on 8 June, but it may be one of them.

1 June 2017

⇨ The above information is reprinted with kind permission from *The Conversation*. Please visit www. theconversation.com for further information.

The national minimum wage and living wage rates

The hourly rate for the minimum wage depends on your age and whether you're an apprentice.

You must be at least:

⇨ school leaving age to get the National Minimum Wage

⇨ aged 25 to get the National Living Wage – the minimum wage will still apply for workers aged 24 and under.

Current rates

These rates are for the National Living Wage and the National Minimum Wage. The rates change every April.

April 2018	
25 and over	£7.83
21 to 24	£7.38
18 to 20	£5.90
Under 18	£4.20
Apprentice	£3.70

Apprentices

Apprentices are entitled to the apprentice rate if they're either:

⇨ aged under 19

⇨ aged 19 or over and in the first year of their apprenticeship.

Example

An apprentice aged 22 in the first year of their apprenticeship is entitled to a minimum hourly rate of £3.70.

Apprentices are entitled to the minimum wage for their age if they both:

⇨ are aged 19 or over

⇨ have completed the first year of their apprenticeship.

Example

An apprentice aged 22 who has completed the first year of their apprenticeship is entitled to a minimum hourly rate of £7.38.

Previous rates

The following rates were for the National Living Wage and the National Minimum Wage from April 2016.

	Apr 2017 – Mar 2018	Oct 2016 – Mar 2017	Apr 2016 – Sept 2016
25 and over	£7.50	£7.20	£7.20
21 to 24	£7.05	£6.95	£6.70
18 to 20	£5.60	£5.55	£5.30
Under 18	£4.05	£4.00	£3.87
Apprentice	£3.50	£3.40	£3.30

Rates before April 2016

The following rates were for the National Minimum Wage before the National Living Wage was introduced. The rates were usually updated every October.

Year	21 and over	18 to 20	Under 18	Apprentice
2015	£6.70	£5.30	£3.87	£3.30
2014	£6.50	£5.13	£3.79	£2.73
2013	£6.31	£5.03	£3.72	£2.68
2012	£6.19	£4.98	£3.68	£2.65

⇨ The above information is reprinted with kind permission from Gov. UK. Please visit www.gov.uk for further information.

Universal Credit: who will win and lose from the new system?

Iain Duncan Smith's welfare project aims to simplify benefits system and ensure that work pays.

The national rollout of Universal Credit began almost exactly a year ago, with first-time claimants being offered the new benefit instead of jobseeker's allowance. But unrolling the system nationwide is moving glacially slow and will take a number of years.

The concept of Universal Credit, first announced in 2010 by Iain Duncan Smith, the Work and Pensions Secretary, enjoyed cross-party support but its implementation has come under fire and cuts to payments have sparked new controversy.

The new single monthly payment is said to mark the biggest overhaul of the benefits system in 60 years. So what difference will it make and when will it come into force?

What is Universal Credit?

It is a new type of financial support for people on a low income or looking for work. The single monthly payment will eventually replace six other benefits and tax credits, including: income-based jobseeker's allowance; income-related employment and support allowance; income support; child tax credit; working tax credit; and housing benefit.

Why is it being introduced?

According to the Government, Universal Credit will bring greater fairness to the welfare system by "ensuring that people are better off in work than on benefits". Duncan Smith says that the old system reduces the financial incentives of taking a job as it is difficult for claimants to take on short-term or part-time work without losing all their benefits at once.

Universal Credit gradually reduces as claimants earn more, with no limits to the number of hours people can work in a week.

In encouraging more people to move into work, it is also intended to reduce the benefits bill – savings which will only be increased by cuts to the payments under the system that were announced last year.

How will it work?

The new system is supposed to be simpler and encourages claimants to take more responsibility for their own money. It will generally be managed online rather than at a job centre and in most cases, a single amount, made up of all the various elements, will be be paid directly into the claimant's bank account each month, rather than weekly or fortnightly. Tenants who need help with rent will be paid directly, rather than the money going straight to their landlord as before. Those applying for universal credit will also have to sign up to a 'claimant commitment' which sets out their responsibilities, such as doing everything they reasonably can to find work. Anyone who fails to stick to the contract without good reason may face sanctions.

When will it be introduced?

Universal Credit is being introduced gradually across different geographical areas and claimant groups, such as single people, couples and families. It was first introduced in selected trial areas in April 2013 and is now being introduced across the country for new unemployment benefit claimants. The roll-out was due to be complete by 2017, but ongoing delays to the programme mean it is now unlikely to be complete before 2021.

Who are the winners and losers?

A report from the Institute of Fiscal Studies (IFS) – that scourge of government fiscal policy after its research was used to corral opposition against cuts to working tax credits last year – has said it's a mixed bag. "An estimated 2.1 million families will face an average loss of £1,600 a year, while 1.8 million will gain an average of £1,500," says the BBC.

In terms of specifics, the institute's figures show 1.1 million homes with no one in paid work will lose out by about £2,300 a year, while 500,000 will gain £1,000. Working single parents are said to face an annual loss of £1,000, while *The Guardian* notes one-earner couples with children would gain more than £500 a year.

How does that compare to its stated aims?

The IFS told the *Daily Telegraph* that "while there will be winners and losers, if you look at the overall structure there are improvements on what we have at the moment". It added that the overall aim of the change was "mostly intact" and that incentives to move people into work remained strong, with most – though not all – keeping more of their earnings once they find employment.

That hasn't satisfied critics, who point to losers among the lowest paid compared to the current system, especially among working families. But the Government has always said no individuals will lose money as a result of the changes, the BBC says, with new claimants to be helped by transitional support.

What other criticism has it faced?

The theory of universal credit won cross-party support, but its rollout has drawn much criticism. Last year, the Commons Public Accounts Committee published a damning report on the programme, describing its implementation as "extraordinarily poor". Margaret Hodge, chairman of the committee, said a "shocking absence" of financial and other internal controls meant that at least £140 million worth of IT assets for the programme will have to be written off and the 2017 target was unlikely to be met. Ministers have since said that new leadership is in place and controls have been strengthened.

This week, the committee issued another report saying the programme was unlikely to complete before 2021 and accused the Department of Work and Pensions of being "evasive" over why it was moving so slowly.

3 February 2016

⇨ The above information is reprinted with kind permission from *The Week*. Please visit www.theweek. co.uk for further information.

© 2018 The Week

What is Universal Credit? Everything you need to know about the UK's biggest ever shake up of benefits

By Jasmin Gray

Universal Credit is a flagship benefits scheme rolling out across the country.

While the Government claims it will leave three million families better off each month, critics – including some Tory MPs – say the move is pushing some of the country's most vulnerable people to the brink.

Either way, the change represents the largest shake up of benefits in the UK in decades.

Here's everything you need to know about Universal Credit.

What is Universal Credit?

Universal Credit is a new means-tested payment being rolled out across the UK in what has been described as "the biggest-ever reform of benefits".

Intended to be simpler than the current system, the single, monthly payment replaces six key benefits and tax credits:

⇨ Child tax credit

⇨ Housing benefit

⇨ Income support

⇨ Income-based jobseeker's allowance

⇨ Income-related employment and support allowance

⇨ Working tax credit.

Who can apply for Universal Credit?

According to the Government, you may be eligible for Universal Credit if you're a low income worker, or you're unemployed.

However, you cannot claim Universal Credit if you:

⇨ are expected to earn more than £338 in the next month

⇨ are self-employed

⇨ have savings of more than £6,000

⇨ are not able to work or look for work due to a health condition or disability

⇨ are in full-time education or training

⇨ are not a British Citizen

⇨ are a homeowner

⇨ are homeless

⇨ are a carer, including if you're a foster carer

⇨ are pregnant or you've had a baby within the last 15 weeks

⇨ are liable to pay child maintenance.

How much is Universal Credit worth?

As Universal Credit is means-tested, the amount you may be eligible to receive is dependent on your circumstances.

The payment is made up of a basic allowance, with extra money dependent on additional elements.

According to hardship charity Turn2Us, basic universal credit allowances are as follows:

⇨ Single claimant aged under 25: £251.77 per month

⇨ Single claimant aged 25 or over: £317.82 per month

⇨ Joint claimants both aged under 25: £395.20 per month

⇨ Joint claimants aged 25 or over: £498.89.

There are then additional elements which can be added to the basic allowance, including a:

⇨ child element

⇨ child-care costs element

- ⇨ limited capability for work element
- ⇨ carer element
- ⇨ housing costs element.

Why is it controversial?

One of the biggest controversies around Universal Credit is that claimants can be forced to wait for up to six weeks without payments when they first apply.

According to activists and critics, this means financially vulnerable people are being pushed into increasingly precarious situations.

While some are left dependent on food banks while they wait for the benefits to be paid, others are being left with rent arrears as they struggle to cover housing costs.

Tory MP Kevin Hollinrake has said Universal Credit was leading people to flock to food banks in record numbers, accusing the Government of "frightening" incompetence.

Hollinrake, who chairs the All Party Parliamentary Committee for poverty, said: "A lot of my work is visiting food banks and most of the problems there are caused by Universal Credit. It's crazy that that is the situation."

He is just one of a dozen Conservative politicians who have called for the rollout of Universal Credit to be paused, according to the *Daily Telegraph*.

One single mother who is currently receiving the benefit told Radio 4's *Today* programme she was forced to turn to loans to feed her children while she waited for the money.

She also criticised the fact that Universal Credit is paid on a monthly basis, rather than weekly or fortnightly like other benefits, saying: "You're living on fresh air and water by the end, clinging on and counting down the days until the next payment is due."

4 October 2017

- ⇨ The above information is reprinted with kind permission from The Huffington Post UK. Please visit www.huffingtonpost.co.uk for further information.

Yes, you're (still) better off working than on benefits

New analysis shows that you're still better off in low paid work than on benefits, but the financial advantages have shrunk for some.

By Chris Goulden

Three years ago I wrote a blog about this, and new analysis shows that you're still better off in low paid work than on benefits, but the financial advantages have shrunk for some. The answer to this lies in improving take-home pay and reducing costs, not more cuts to out-of-work benefits.

A single person without children is better off in work than three years ago…

Let's first look at Jake, a 25-year-old single man seeking work. Using data from the JRF Minimum Income Calculator, if he rents a modest one-roomed flat, he will receive each week:

- ⇨ Jobseekers Allowance of £73.10
- ⇨ Housing Benefit of £86.11 (enough to cover most but not all the £89.70 rent on his flat)
- ⇨ Council Tax Support of £13.40 (enough to cover most but not all his £15.76 bill)
- ⇨ leaving a total disposable income of **£67.15**.

That's over £3 a week LESS in absolute terms than three years ago. The gap between his housing costs and the benefits to cover them has grown and he's far short of a decent living standard. However, if Jake gets a job full-time on the minimum wage (£7.50 per hour), then he'd:

- ⇨ earn £281.25 gross a week
- ⇨ pay £12.14 in income tax and £14.91 in National Insurance

- ⇨ get nothing at all in Housing Benefit, tax credits or council tax support, as this level of earnings is too high to be eligible
- ⇨ have a total disposable income of **£148.74** (after paying rent and council tax).

That's only an extra £82 for 37½ hours a week of hard work, but £20 more than in 2014. This isn't adjusted for the increase in prices since then but it shows the gap between benefits and work for single, childless adults has gone quickly upwards. That's due to freezes or cuts in benefits as well as the introduction of the National Living Wage.

Of course, Jake pays more in tax and NI than in 2014 because of the minimum wage hike – he's earning more and better off despite paying around £280 extra a year in tax. If Jake was switched onto Universal Credit (UC), he'd be no worse or better off financially as it basically mirrors the old system for simpler cases like this (notwithstanding issues with the administration of UC).

A family of four with one worker is worse off in work than three years ago…

But how does Jake's experience compare with the way families with children have fared over the last few years? Mr and Mrs Clark, parents of two primary school-aged children, would receive these benefits each week if they were both out of work:

- ⇨ JSA £114.85
- ⇨ Child Benefit £34.40

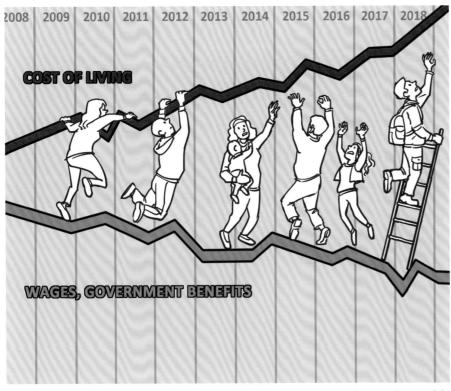

2008 | 2009 | 2010 | 2011 | 2012 | 2013 | 2014 | 2015 | 2016 | 2017 | 2018

COST OF LIVING

WAGES, GOVERNMENT BENEFITS

- ⇨ Child Tax Credit £117.18

- ⇨ Housing Benefit £91.05 (covering all the rent on their three-bed council house, unless in some circumstances they're subject to the bedroom tax)

- ⇨ Council Tax Support £20.83 (covering most of their £24.51 bill)

- ⇨ leaving a disposable income of **£262.75**.

If Mrs Clark gets a full-time job on the National Living Wage, then they would:

- ⇨ get gross earnings of £281.25 (the same as Jake)

- ⇨ pay income tax of £7.73 and NI of £14.91 (income tax is £230 a year lower than Jake because of the transferable Marriage Allowance)

- ⇨ get Working Tax Credit of £26.87 and the same level of CB and CTC as when out of work

- ⇨ get a much-reduced HB of £8.46 (and no CTS)

- ⇨ leaving a disposable income of **£330.06**

That's an additional £67 disposable income each week from one of them working full-time – about £6 less than three years ago and less in absolute terms than Jake (who gets £82). The incentive to work has gotten worse because of: the tapering of in-work benefits with rising earnings, a small additional cut in Housing Benefit and an increase in NI paid. The rise in the minimum wage, less income tax paid and slight rises in child-related benefits are not enough to offset this. In contrast, the disposable income of the Clarks when out of work is virtually the same as three years ago – but they would still be around £200 short each week of what the public think a family of four needs for a decent living standard.

If the Clarks moved onto UC, it would make barely any difference if they were both still unemployed – in fact, they'd be 13p a week worse off. But being in work on UC would leave them around £35 a week better off than on the old system; that's over £1,800 a year. Unfortunately, they are in the minority as many other family types will be relatively worse off on UC, given the cuts that have been made to it.

Still better off working than on benefits (mostly)…

The fortunes of Jake and the Clarks have diverged. Financial incentives in the non-UC system have worsened for families to move from zero to one worker but have improved for single childless adults. UC doesn't help Jake but its more generous treatment of the Clarks boosts their income considerably.

While these simple examples show that the system is still designed to make people better off when working, whether on UC or tax credits, there are additional complexities that could undermine this. That includes travel and other costs associated with working, expensive childcare and housing that might not be fully covered by benefits, or passported benefits that can be lost when people move into a job. These can all cut into the narrow margin of the extra £70 or £80 per week that these two households might typically see in their pockets when working full-time on the NLW.

Given how low the levels already are, it would be hard to argue that out of work benefits should be cut back further to increase the incentives to work. Action should be taken on reducing the cost of living (especially housing and childcare) and improving earnings, by ending the benefit freeze, restoring work allowances in UC, continuing to ramp up the NLW, reducing taxes on income and improving opportunities to progress in work.

19 October 2017

- ⇨ The above information is reprinted with kind permission from The Joseph Rowntree Foundation. Please visit www.jrf.org.uk for further information.

"Forgotten unemployed": 300,000 jobless people in UK not claiming benefits

Unemployed people and low earners – mainly older women and younger men – are missing out on £21.9 million in benefits each week, Resolution Foundation think tank finds

By May Bulman

Around 300,000 people who are "forgotten unemployed" or on a low income are missing out on financial support they are entitled to, according to a new report.

The group, made up mainly of older people, especially women aged 55 to 64, and younger men, were not claiming unemployment benefits worth at least £73 a week, the Resolution Foundation found.

This amounts to a weekly total of £21.9 million in benefits that goes unclaimed.

Most of those missing out on financial support were jobless, prompting the think tank to dub them the "forgotten unemployed".

However, a significant minority were in work and entitled to claim universal credit or Jobseeker's Allowance, according to the report.

It is possible for someone to claim Jobseeker's Allowance if they are not working or employed for less than 16 hours a week and if their partner is either not working or working fewer than 24 hours a week.

An individual's entitlement to the benefit ends once their income reaches £78 a week.

Under Universal Credit, which will eventually replace Jobseekers Allowance, that point is £116, or higher if the claimant also receives support for their rent.

The Resolution Foundation has said the Department for Work and Pensions (DWP) must do more to examine the reasons why so many eligible people do not claim.

As Universal Credit is currently being rolled out, it said this would be a good time to do this.

The new benefit system could provide a "much needed refocus" on groups at the edges of the labour market who need support, the think tank said.

It also suggested universal credit could still miss some key groups who currently do not claim support.

The Government should look into linking of household survey data, with more detail of an individual's background and administrative data, it said.

This could "plug the gaps" and provide a better understanding of those who need support and those who do not claim, it added.

"Over the last 20 years, a growing number of unemployed people are not claiming unemployment benefits," said David Finch, senior economic analyst at the Resolution Foundation.

"Policy makers have generally been pretty relaxed about this gap, assuming that it is largely due to people finding new work very quickly or having other sources of financial support at home.

"But while there are good reasons for some people not to claim benefits, there are also around 300,000 forgotten unemployed people who are falling through the cracks and not getting the financial support that they need and are entitled to."

A DWP spokesperson said: "Anyone who believes they're entitled to out-of-work benefits should contact Jobcentre Plus – online, over the phone or by visiting their local branch."

They added that "advisers and work coaches are on hand to help people claim what they are entitled to, and can signpost to other support options available."

2 January 2018

⇨ The above information is reprinted with kind permission from *The Independent.* Please visit www.independent.co.uk for further information.

The gender pay gap – what is it and what affects it?

As Jane Austen (almost) said: "it is a truth universally acknowledged that men (generally) get paid more than women."

But do they get paid more than women for doing the same work? That is harder to answer.

The data published today in the *Annual Survey of Hours and Earnings* (ASHE) will give us the most up-to-date information on the pay gap between men and women.

The gender pay gap has fallen but remains steady in recent years

The gender pay gap for full-time employees in 2016 was 9.4%.

This means average pay for full-time female employees was 9.4% lower than for full-time male employees. This gap is down from 17.4% in 1997.

The gap for all employees (full-time and part-time) has reduced from 19.3% in 2015 to 18.1% in 2016. This gap is down from 27.5% in 1997.

Reasons for the gap

The main factors explaining why women tend to earn less than men are:

⇨ part-time work

⇨ type of occupation

⇨ having and caring for children.

Part-time work

Part-time workers – both men and women – earn less, on average, per hour than their full-time counterparts.

A much higher proportion of women work part-time – 41%, compared with only 12% of men. This is why the gap for all employees – full-time and part-time together – is higher than for full-time employees.

Interestingly, the gender pay gap for part-time employees alone was minus 6.0% in 2016. This means female part-time employees earned 6.0% more than male part-time employees.

Occupation

Another factor that affects the gender pay gap is that women tend to work in occupations which offer lower salaries. The size of the gender pay gap also varies between occupations.

The chart below shows a higher proportion of women than men working in sectors such as administration and caring, which tend to be lower paid.

Having and caring for children

When looking at the differences in pay by age group for full-time employees, the gap is relatively small up to and including those aged 30 to 39.

From 40 upwards, the gap is much wider. This is likely to be connected to women taking time out of the labour market to have children.

Taking full-time and part-time employees together, for all age groups from 22 to 29 upwards, the gap is wider than for full-time employees alone. This indicates that, in these age groups, more women are working part-time in jobs that tend to be lower paid.

Having children may also change what women want from a job. The American economist Claudia Goldin sees women pursuing "temporal flexibility" as "perhaps the most powerful explanation for the gender pay gap". What this means is women are more likely to want the ability to work flexible hours, or to work at home, or to complete a project outside a tight schedule.

26 October 2016

⇨ The above information is reprinted with kind permission from The Office for National Statistics. Please visit www.ons.gov.uk for further information.

© Crown copyright 2018

Part-time work
Percentage of men and women who work part-time, UK, April – June 2016

41% of women work part-time

12% of men work part-time

Source: Labour Force Survey

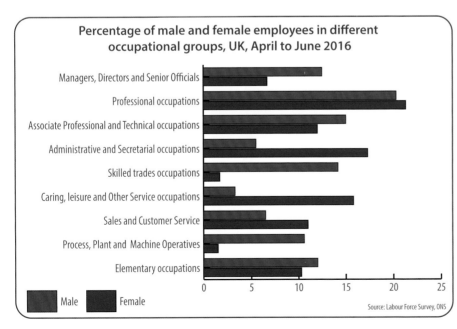

Percentage of male and female employees in different occupational groups, UK, April to June 2016

- Managers, Directors and Senior Officials
- Professional occupations
- Associate Professional and Technical occupations
- Administrative and Secretarial occupations
- Skilled trades occupations
- Caring, leisure and Other Service occupations
- Sales and Customer Service
- Process, Plant and Machine Operatives
- Elementary occupations

■ Male ■ Female

Source: Labour Force Survey, ONS

How early career women help to open up the gender pay gap

An article from **The Conversation.**

THE CONVERSATION

Julie Davies, HR Subject Group Leader, University of Huddersfield and David Fahey, Researcher – The Psychology of Executive Pay, University of Huddersfield

Perhaps Gary Lineker is worth more than Clare Balding? After all, the former footballer fronts the BBC's coverage of the world's most popular sport. Balding, on the other hand, presents the BBC countryside radio programme *Ramblings* and the BBC faith programme *Good Morning Sunday*, alongside other jobs for BBC Sport. In truth, though, the kerfuffle over the BBC gender pay gap is a distraction, and part of a wider trend towards public sector bashing.

Research suggests that the real issue behind gender pay gaps is that women too readily accept low pay offers. And the cost of not negotiating job offers is compounded significantly during a career. In her book, *Women Don't Ask,* Linda Babcock reported that only seven per cent of women negotiate, compared with 57 per cent of men. Those who did negotiate gained at least a seven per cent higher salary. This will clearly accumulate over a lifetime. It appears that many women just assume their hard work will naturally be rewarded.

So are women just naïve or lacking self-belief? Often it doesn't cross their minds to question an initial offer. Carol Frohlinger, Managing Partner at consultancy and training firm, Negotiating Women, says only 16 per cent of women will always seize the opportunity to negotiate pay when the opportunity arises. In their research, economists Andreas Leibbrandt and John List found that women were more likely to negotiate if they are aware this option is open to them. Whether those offering jobs would ever want to make that clear is another question altogether.

Managing expectations

Some women may feel it is vulgar to discuss gender pay gaps, as Kate Winslet has suggested. Many are anxious about blowing an offer completely by negotiating. Some fear they will be penalised for asking for more money when they also need to ask for flexibility over childcare – for which they may also be punished. They feel grateful for flexibility in conditions and are willing to prioritise this over pay. Women also feel uncomfortable about taking full credit, opting to talk instead about the team's rather than their own contribution.

David Fahey, a consultant and part-time PhD student at Huddersfield Business School, has observed this among executive women in the UK over the past decade. He says that they often comment in salary negotiations: "I know my salary is below market rate but I'm being challenged intellectually, learning a lot." They sometimes say they "haven't really thought about the salary". The argument should go that big challenges justify bigger salaries.

Men tend to be more assertive. If expectations fall short, men are more

likely to leave the table. Curiously, in an article on gender differences in tough negotiations, Sara Solnick even found that women offer larger salaries to men. Perhaps women can learn something on assertiveness from Amy Cuddy's popular TED talk?

In Hollywood, even extraordinarily successful women appear to lack confidence. Meryl Streep recalls how the initial offer for her to act in *The Devil Wears Prada* was a dramatic moment:

"The offer was to my mind ... not perhaps reflective of my actual value to the project. There was my 'goodbye moment', and then they doubled the offer. I was 55, and I had just learned... how to deal on my own behalf"

Taking responsibility

The common discourse around the gender pay gap absolves women of any responsibility for creating it. Both male and female leaders, HR professionals and especially early career women must engage in uncomfortable conversations if they are serious about tackling it.

We do not suggest that if women simply did what men do the pay gap would vanish. Jawad Syed, Dean of Dawood School of Business, Lahore University of Management Sciences and a gender scholar, has noted historical gender stereotyping remains prevalent and life cycle differences between the sexes are not yet accommodated and valued.

And it is hard to spot that young women have failed to negotiate early pay deals properly until it is too late. If they take time out for childcare, then the accumulated pay disparity may worsen as they miss annual reviews or have gaps in experience come pay review time. An early career lawyer

breaking into a male-dominated firm might be tempted to thank her lucky stars and take whatever she's offered. You might expect lawyers to be natural negotiators, but it is revealing to find that three former female partners have filed a US$100 million lawsuit against US law firm Chadbourne & Parke for gender pay disparity. Chadbourne is contesting the claim.

The more male-dominated the context and the greater the demands in terms of hours and travel, the harder it may be for women to ask for more pay. Well-educated and well-qualified women frequently assume pay is just

on the basis of merit, a myth that the sociologists Stephen J. McNamee and Robert K. Miller, Jr discredited in their 2004 book.

Gender pay differentials are not just happening among Hollywood and BBC celebrities. It happens at all levels and is taking new forms as business models change in the gig economy. Clearly, more transparent internal systems and legislation on mandatory, granular gender gap reporting would be helpful in addressing this issue, as we see in Nordic countries.

The gender gap is gouged out by an incremental process as women's salaries are repeatedly undercut during their careers. Over successive jobs, and for a variety of reasons, women can be too ready to accept the offer on the table. Each time they move, their pay parity with men can worsen, particularly when the new pay is related to their current salary package. This is also compounded generally by worse pay for mothers and older women.

The quiet scandal, though, is why women consistently feel that they need to accept low offers. We should be discussing behavioural economics rather than bashing the BBC. The focus instead should be on supporting women to negotiate fairer pay.

27 July 2017

⇨ The above information is reprinted with kind permission from *The Conversation*. Please visit www.theconversation.com for further information.

Flexible working not just for mothers, says largest ever study of UK workforce

By Richard Jones

Flexible working is not just for mothers, the largest and most focused review of Britain's permanent workforce has found.

New research from flexible working experts Timewise has revealed that almost nine in ten (87 per cent) of the UK's full-time workforce either currently work flexibly or would like to do so. 84 per cent of the men surveyed work flexibly or wish to do so compared to 91 per cent of women.

It polled 3,000 UK adults on how they work, how important flexible working is as a benefit, and their motivations for needing or wanting working patterns that don't fit the 9-to-5 mould.

Flexible working was defined as either part-time, or if full-time, a work pattern that involves reduced hours, shift choices or the ability to work at home for some, or all, of the working week.

The survey wants to "bust the mum myth" and do away with preconceptions that flexible working is only for women with children, or those with parenting responsibilities.

It found that millennials are leading the pack when it comes to new ways of working, with seven in ten (73 per cent) of those aged 18 to 34 who are working full-time, doing so flexibly. Of the 37 per cent of full-time workers who do not work flexibly, 64 per cent would prefer to. The research also showed that 72 per cent of those aged over 55 either currently work flexibly, would like to work flexibly or would prefer to work part-time.

The main reasons put forward as to why workers would wish to work flexibly include increased control over their work–life balance, reducing their energy-sapping commute, allowing more time for leisure and study, and more opportunities to care for children and other dependents.

Unfortunately, employers still have a long way to go to satisfy the flexible working desires of the nation, with less than one in ten quality jobs – paying £20,000 FTE or above – advertised as being open to flexible working options.

Karen Mattison MBE, joint CEO of Timewise, says: "The fact that flexible working has been seen as a women's issue has not done women or businesses any favours. Today's new research shows once and for all, that flexible working is a preferred way of working for both men and women at all stages of their working lives.

"Today's workforce not only want it, but they expect it. It's time for businesses to get smarter and use flexibility as a tool to attract and keep the best people. Those who lag behind in adapting how they hire, will risk losing out on millions of skilled workers".

Every employee in the UK has the statutory right to request flexible working after 26 weeks of employment. And yet a Trades Union Congress (TUC) survey of 1,000 parents earlier this month found that two out of five low-paid young parents who ask for flexible work arrangements are 'penalised' as a result – either through worse shifts, fewer hours or even losing their job.

Multinational professional services firm, EY, have supported the new findings and flexible working patterns. On the report, Lynn Rattigan, Chief Operating Officer at EY UK & Ireland, says: "The working world is being transformed by advances in technology with the rise of the gig economy and a flexible working policy is no longer enough. Smart companies are already adapting by hiring flexibly, designing roles and working patterns creatively, and using more contingent workers – overall, establishing an agile working workforce and culture fit for the future."

19 September 2017

⇨ The above information is reprinted with kind permission from *The Telegraph*. Please visit www.telegraph.co.uk for further information.

Want more women in top positions? Provide them with more flexibility at work

An article from **The Conversation.**

Heejung Chung, Senior Lecturer in Sociology and Social Policy, University of Kent

THE CONVERSATION

The recent BBC report on the pay of its top earners laid bare the disparities between men and women's earnings. But it should come as no surprise. The gender pay gap has been stubbornly stagnant over the past decade. According to the EU (which calculates the gap based on hourly pay differences between men and women), men earn around 20% more. And the UK's official statistics group, which calculates the pay gap of full-time earnings, men earn an average of about 10% more than women.

One core reason for this difference is the tendency for women to drop out of the labour market or move into (bad and low-paid) part-time jobs after having children. Employment data makes this clear.

For example, in 2015, 85% of women between the ages of 25–49 without children were employed, exactly the same proportion as childless men employed in the same age group. But women are likely to drop out of the labour market or reduce their hours after childbirth, while men are more likely to increase their hours and increase their labour market participation.

The stats show that there is a sharp drop in the employment rate of women with children – to 71% – while the employment rate of fathers rises to more than 90%. Further, only 16% of all women between the ages of 25–49 without dependent children worked part-time, while this proportion more than triples for women in the same age group with children to 52%.

It isn't just about working part-time but the quality of part-time work is also a factor. It is widely known that women usually switch to lower-paying, lower-quality jobs when moving into part-time work, due to the lack of high-quality well-paid part-time jobs in the UK.

So the question arises: what can we do to help women maintain their working patterns after childbirth, without sacrificing their careers? My research into flexible working arrangements shows that they can help women maintain their working hours and stay in employment.

Introducing flexitime

Obviously the more flexibility you have at work the better you are able to shape work around family demands. I myself am a good example of this. Coming back to work from having taken six months of maternity leave after the birth of my daughter, I would not have been able to go back to work full-time if it wasn't for the flexibility I had at work. Given the great amount of freedom you have as an academic to work whenever and wherever you want (within limits), I was able to work full-time by working from home and catching up on work during the weekends and evenings when my baby was asleep or I had other childcare support available. It was hard and I lost a lot of sleep – but through such flexibility I was able to maintain my research career.

I wondered whether similar patterns could be observed for other women in the UK. To investigate, my colleague Mariska van der Horst and I used a data set of 40,000 households to see whether being able to have control over when you work and where you work influences women's likelihood of remaining in employment and not reducing their working hours significantly (of more than four hours) after the birth of their children. The results were remarkable.

In our research, which was published in the journal *Human Relations*, we found that women who were able to use flexitime were only half as likely to reduce their working hours after the birth of their child. This effect was especially the case for the women who used flexitime prior to the birth of their child as well as after.

In the overall sample, more than half the women reduced their working hours after the birth of their child. But less than a quarter of the women who were able to use flexitime reduced their hours, with similar results for women who were able to work from home if they wanted to. This shows that, given the chance to work flexibly, many women would stay in work and maintain their hours and their pay after having children.

As I've found in previous research, not all jobs allow for flexible work arrangements – and they are not necessarily provided to those in most need of them. Rather, they tend to be given more to high-skilled, higher educated workers in supervisory roles. Another recent study found that a large number of mothers are forced to leave their jobs after flexible working requests were turned down.

It is not only a matter of justice but also a matter of society's economic prosperity and development to ensure that women are able to remain in the labour market across different stages of the life cycle, including childbirth. The right to flexible working is crucial if we are to tackle the problem of gender inequality in the labour market – especially when it comes to having a balance at the top of the career ladder.

18 August 2017

Zero-hours contracts "here to stay" as figures show young hit by 15% rise in "insecure work" deals

By Graeme Demianyk

Young people have been hit hardest by a sharp rise in the number of workers on zero-hours contracts.

The Office for National Statistics figure has leapt by 104,000 to 801,000, official figures have revealed, despite the economy improving.

The Labour Party said the 15 per cent rise in the final quarter of 2015 underlined a "crisis of insecure work under the Tories".

An analysis by the Resolution Foundation think tank found the increase came largely from workers aged 16–24, suggesting that the young are being hit hardest.

It said zero-hours contracts are "here to stay, whatever the economic weather". The share of workers on these contracts grew despite when pay is improving and employment growing.

Owen Smith, Labour's Shadow Work and Pensions Secretary, said: "The scale of the crisis of insecure work under the Tories is getting worse with every passing week.

"Before the election they promised to act on zero-hours contracts, but these numbers show that was nothing more than words. Spiralling numbers of British workers cannot be certain where their next day's work is coming from, making it virtually impossible to plan finances and family life.

"While from this April their cuts to Universal Credit will take an average of £1,600 from over two million low and middle paid working families, hitting people in insecure low paid work hardest.

"The test for this Budget is whether it can start to lay the foundations for a modern economy. So the Government must act on this crisis by reversing the Universal Credit cuts and properly clamp downing on exploitative zero-hour contracts."

Laura Gardiner, senior research and policy analyst at the Resolution Foundation, said: "As a share of the workforce, the number of people on zero-hours contracts continues to rise despite the record employment rate and the long-overdue pay recovery last year. It's increasingly clear that ZHCs are here to stay, whatever the economic weather.

"While some workers value the flexibility they provide, others struggle to manage their fluctuating pay levels week by week and find it hard to budget and put any money aside as savings. This explains why one in three workers on a ZHC want more hours.

"While zero-hours contracts still make up a comparatively small, albeit growing, part of the labour market, it is still crucial that policy makers consider the effect of unstable employment on both workers and the economy, while ensuring the employment rate continues to reach record highs."

But business leaders urged caution, pointing to the increase in the number of employees saying they were on zero-hours contracts.

Seamus Nevin, Head of Employment and Skills at the Institute of Directors, said: "Today's figures will inevitably provoke a storm, but before jumping to conclusions, we need to look at the facts. Firstly, the Office for National Statistics is very clear that there has not necessarily been an increase in the number of people on zero-hours contracts.

"It is likely that some people are now just more aware of the name because of press coverage and so the level of under-reporting has been reduced. Indeed, ONS figures show that the number of businesses using zero-hours contracts might actually be falling.

"More to the point, it is important to note that the vast majority (two-thirds) of people on zero-hours contracts say they are happy with their employment terms and do not want to work more hours. For students, elderly workers in semi-retirement, and people with childcare responsibilities, zero-hours contracts offer much needed flexibility that they can't get with other forms of employment.

"Many of the issues campaigners had against zero-hours contracts have now been resolved. The last government correctly banned exclusivity clauses, which said that an employee could only work for one company at a time.

"One of the reasons that UK employment figures remained so impressive despite the financial crisis is because employers have been able to adopt zero-hours contracts instead of having to make redundancies. The bottom line is that flexibility is a good thing, and the current balance is working well for both workers and employers."

9 March 2016

⇨ The above information is reprinted with kind permission from The Huffington Post UK. Please visit www.huffingtonpost.co.uk for further information.

Being on a zero-hours contract is bad for your health

Young adults who are employed on zero-hours contracts are less likely to be in good health, and are at higher risk of poor mental health than workers with stable jobs.

Researchers from the Centre for Longitudinal Studies at UCL Institute of Education (IOE) analysed data on more than 7,700 people living in England who were born in 1989–90 and are being followed by a study called Next Steps.

They found that at age 25, people on zero-hours contracts and those who were unemployed were less likely to report feeling healthy, compared to those in more secure employment.

Those with zero-hours contracts were also at greater risk of reporting symptoms of psychological distress. However, young adults who were unemployed were more than twice as likely to suffer from mental ill health compared to those who were in work.

And, although shift workers were at no greater risk than those working regular hours to be in poor health, they were more likely to have psychological problems.

The lead author, Dr Morag Henderson, said: "Millennials have faced a number of challenges as they entered the world of work. They joined the labour market at the height of the most recent financial crisis and faced higher than ever university fees and student loan debt.

"There is evidence that those with a precarious relationship to the labour market, such as shift workers, zero-hours contract holders and the unemployed are more at risk of poor mental health and physical health than their peers.

"One explanation for these findings is that financial stress or the stress associated with having a low-status

job increases the risk of poor mental health. It may also be that the worry of having no work or irregular work triggers physical symptoms of stress, including chest pain, headaches and muscle tension."

Two-thirds of 25-year-olds were employed full-time, one in eight (12%) were employed part time, and seven per cent were unemployed. Around a quarter (23%) worked shifts, and five per cent had zero-hours contracts.

By occupation, the largest proportion of young adults (15%) were in professional roles, such as teachers, engineers and accountants. A further 14 per cent had professional support roles, including paramedics, librarians and pharmacists, nine per cent were in administrative or secretarial occupations and eight per cent had manual roles, such as general labourers and forestry workers.

The findings took into account background factors such as gender, ethnicity, social class, prior mental health, sleep duration, frequency of exercise and weight.

Craig Thorley, Senior Research Fellow at the Institute for Public Policy Research (IPPR), said: "Efforts to improve the UK's mental health must recognise the important relationship between health and work. More people than ever are working on zero-hours contracts in the UK, and this new data shows this to be contributing to poorer mental health among younger workers.

"Government and employers must work together to promote better quality jobs which enhance, rather than damage, mental health and well-being. Without this, we risk seeing increased demand for mental health services, reduced productivity, and more young people moving on to out-of-work sickness benefits."

5 July 2017

⇨ The above information is reprinted with kind permission from University College London. Please visit www.ucl.ac.uk for further information.

Why zero-hours contracts are becoming increasingly popular

By Nav Sekhon-Sharma

There is so much hype in the media about how zero-hours contracts (also known as contingent work contracts) are the enemy, but are they really as bad as we're being led to believe?

According to the BBC, new figures based on an analysis from the Office for National Statistics, reveal that 105,000 more people were on contracts that do not guarantee work in 2016, compared with the same period in 2015.

Over the years, many people have called for there to be a ban on zero-hours contracts: however, in June 2016, Prime Minister David Cameron refused calls to ban zero-hours contracts insisting: "some people want to have the choice".

Age, Gender and employment status

A survey undertaken by the Office for National Statistics states that people on zero-hours contracts are most likely to be young, part-time working women, or people in full-time education.

903,000 people surveyed throughout the UK were on a zero-hours contract. The pie chart opposite shows how the number of people on zero-hours contracts in the UK is split by age.

Advantages of zero-hours contracts

The rhetoric tells us that people on zero-hours contracts are underpaid, don't have the same entitlement as others and lack job security.

Whilst we're constantly talking about the negatives of zero-hours contracts, we tend to forget that a large number of people actually appreciate this type of contract for a variety of reasons:

➡ Flexibility for parents with children;

➡ Flexibility for people who want to work in other places;

➡ Retired people who want to get out of the house for just a few hours a week;

➡ Employees who receive employment rights such as annual leave, do not have to accept work offered;

➡ According to Fairwork.gov, casual employees in Australia receive a higher hourly pay rate than equivalent full-time or part-time employees.

We spoke to a 29-year-old nurse from London about her experience of working on a zero-hours contract in retail part-time:

"I was extremely happy with being on a zero-hours contract at a large multinational retailer, as it gave me the flexibility of working in other places whilst not being tied down to one company. I worked for this retailer for seven years; however, last year the company sent me an email to say my contract had been terminated as I hadn't worked at the store for over a year.

"I had no written evidence to say if I didn't work a certain amount of time my contract would be terminated, which was appalling and not something you would expect from such a large high street retailer."

We also spoke to another source who works at a large UK airport:

"A lot of my colleagues are on zero-hours contracts and it suits them because some of them have children so they can choose hours to fit around their lifestyles.

"Also, some of my colleagues are retired and only want to work a few hours a week just to get them out the house, so this type of contract is perfect for them."

There's no doubt that many people are happy with working on zero-hours contracts; however, employees do need to be made aware of the rules beforehand.

If zero-hours contracts were banned, it would be difficult for older members of a company's workforce to embrace this change, given the commitments and lifestyle choices they've already made.

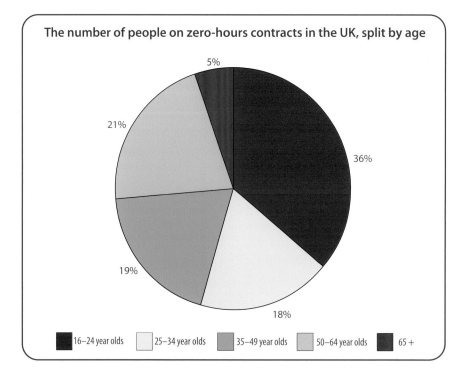

The number of people on zero-hours contracts in the UK, split by age

5%

21%

36%

19%

18%

■ 16–24 year olds ☐ 25–34 year olds ▨ 35–49 year olds ▨ 50–64 year olds ■ 65 +

Is the younger workforce less committed to work?

Do zero-hours contracts actually mirror the work ethic of the younger generation?

From research undertaken we found that Generation Z is much less likely to burden themselves with the types of commitments previous generations would; for example, loans and mortgages.

So, it doesn't naturally follow that Generation Z is less committed to work, but it does mean they are more relaxed about it. This, in-turn, allows for some flexibility in their lives.

Unions are unhappy, but do unions actually represent the demographic most affected by the increasing numbers of zero-hours contracts?

Unions have recently been voicing their concerns about zero-hours contracts; however, whilst they were at the forefront in the 1970s when employees expected a 'job for life', they've since declined in membership and are lacking in relevance.

The U.S. Bureau of Labor Statistics reported the percentage of wage and salary workers who were members of unions was 10.7 per cent in 2016, down 0.4 percentage from 2015. The number of wage and salary workers belonging to unions, at 14.6 million in 2016, declined by 240,000 from 2015. It is evident there is a decline in membership as unions and demographics split for membership.

The majority of workers on zero-hours contracts are content with their hours

Acting Chief Economist at the CIPD, Ian Brinkley, speaks about zero-hours contracts on CIPD Community and in a survey undertaken, found that around 30% of people on these contracts wanted more hours, which demonstrates that the majority are content with the hours that they work.

He also found that only 15% of people on zero-hours contracts want a new job compared to 5% of those in other contracts.

The Independent discusses how the charity Centrepoint claims zero-hours contracts are "trapping young people in homelessness" and landlords prefer tenants on benefits

The charity Centrepoint told *The Independent* that 16–25-year-olds on zero-hours contracts are likely to be saddled with rent arrears, forcing them to be evicted.

They claim that research undertaken suggested landlords would prefer to take on a tenant that was on benefits rather than someone on a zero-hours contract due to the uncertainty of the amount of money they would earn each month.

A new business starting up would majorly benefit from a workforce on a zero-hours contract

There's no doubt that a start-up would benefit hugely from a workforce on zero-hours contracts: as their business grew, they would incur lower overheads yet still have a skilled resource that you can call upon when needed. With the expectations, the younger generations are bringing with them to the workplace, this more flexible approach fits perfectly, and takes the current demands from Generation Z for a flexible 40-hour week to a whole new level!

In summary

Zero-hours contracts have always had a bad public reputation, but evidence suggests a more nuanced policy response, rather than the outright ban that some have advocated. As the CIPD has argued, the promotion of best practice around the use of zero-hours contracts and the treatment of zero-hours contract workers remains a key means of addressing shortcomings while continuing to offer flexible work options for those who want them.

Employers also benefit from this approach to work, as a more flexible workforce can be called on when needed, rather than being on the payroll the entire time.

We need to stop vilifying zero-hours contracts, and start supporting them as an alternative that provides flexible, paid employment for growing numbers of people around the world.

The 'job for life' is out, and the 'flexible, global workforce' is in.

13 March 2017

⇨ The above information is reprinted with kind permission from REPL Group Worldwide Ltd. Please visit www.replgroup.com for further information.

Work–life balance supports can improve employee well-being

Study by University of Leicester and Norwich Business School reveals how flexible working arrangements can increase satisfaction and reduce anxiety and depression

Professor Stephen Wood, University of Leicester, School of Business

Work–life balance supports provided by employers, often known as flexible working arrangements, can have a significant effect on employees who use them, a new study has found.

Flexible working arrangements include flexitime, job sharing, moving from full-time to part-time working, compressing working hours, home working, working only in school term, paid leave to care for a dependent in an emergency.

Now new research based on a large national survey by Professor Stephen Wood at the University of Leicester School of Business and Kevin Daniels and Chidi Ogbonnaya at Norwich Business School, concludes that work–life balance supports can succeed in improving the well-being of those that use them.

Work–life balance supports are commonly thought to enable employees to better juggle the demands of care and domestic responsibilities and to reduce the demands of work, through reducing workloads, interruptions to work and commuting times, and better prioritisation of work, time management and completion rates.

The authors find, however, that these are not the main reasons for the improved well-being. The novelty of the research is in showing that it is firstly the increased job autonomy that using work–life balance supports provides for employees and secondly an enhanced perception that their management are supportive that explains the well-being effect.

Work–life balance supports increase autonomy in a number of ways, the researchers say. In order to accommodate employees' use of such supports, managers may design work so employees have more discretion over how they prioritise tasks or the methods of fulfilling them. Employees using such supports may become more conscious of time and the need to use it effectively. This may in itself create a sense of increased autonomy, of being more in charge of their lives and having the energy and time to develop their work roles and having more "thinking time", so the authors argue.

As is most pronounced in home-working, employees may also have less contact with their superiors and this may have often quite subtle effects on employees' sense of autonomy. For example, as employees on flexitime may not regularly arrive at work at the same time as their supervisor they are not reminded first thing every day of his/her controlling presence.

Using work–life balance supports may strengthen employees' sense that their employer is fair and cares

for them for two main reasons. First, managers whose subordinates or peers use work–life balance supports may be more inclined to allow or develop informal arrangements with their staff to aid the integration of work and non-work obligations and cope with emergencies because work–life balance supports signal to managers that the organisation values helping workers to cope with such obligations.

Second, work–life balance supports also have a symbolic effect on all employees, signalling that their employer cares for them and that management is supportive of them but this is greater amongst those that use the supports. Through use the symbolic effect becomes less of a substitute for real knowledge of the employer's intentions and more a concrete appreciation of management's commitment. This gives greater credence to judgements about whether the employer is returning the employees' commitment and hence adhering to their side of the bargain.

These factors have a direct impact on well-being but also have an indirect effect through reducing the extent to which work interferes with family and other non-work activities. The increased job autonomy may, for example, enable employees to work more effectively – they can solve problems when they occur and without having to refer to a supervisor – and this means they may not bring unsolved problems home or be stressed by them.

Professor Wood said: "The implication of our findings for employers is that use of work–life balance supports should be used where appropriate. They are a readily implementable means by which an employer can support – and be seen to be supportive

of – employees' needs, and improve the support and job autonomy they experience.

"Our results show that we should certainly not dismiss these supports as having no positive effect even if demands on employees stay the same or even increase. But, perhaps organisations should also tackle directly the adverse effects of increased job demands on well-being,

both in general and that may result from the use of work–life balance supports."

Kevin Daniels emphasised how: "Job autonomy should be treated as a work–life balance support in its own right, and the way that core work–life balance supports can increase this autonomy illustrates how the design of work tasks is not fixed or prescribed

absolutely by the employer, and wider organisational policies and employees themselves shape them."

53% of employees used one or more of work–life balance supports. In the majority of these cases employees use only one support (36% of the sample in the total sample in this survey and 62% of those who used the supports). The use reflects needs as well as the availability of practices as around half of workplaces either had no such supports (26%) or none (25%).

Data used are from one element of 2011 Britain's 2011 Workplace Employment Relations Survey (2011 WERS) which includes a management survey in which managers were interviewed in workplaces and a questionnaire survey of employees completed in the workplaces included in the core element of 2011 WERS. The employee-level data for 2011 WERS were collected through a self-completion questionnaire distributed to 25 randomly-selected employees at workplaces where management interviews were undertaken. The median number of respondents in sampled workplaces was 12, and the range was five–24. Managers gave permission for interviewers to select a sample for the survey of employees in 2,170 workplaces (81% of those where management surveys were conducted). Interviewers then placed a total of 44,371 questionnaires in these workplaces. 21,981 were returned, which represented a response rate of 50% among all sampled employees. The research is reported in S. Wood, K. Daniels, and C. Ogbonnaya, Work-Nonwork Supports, Job Control, Work-Nonwork Conflict, and Well-Being. *International Journal of Human Resource Management*. DOI: 10.1080/09585192.2017.1423102

19 January 2018

⇨ The above information is reprinted with kind permission from Professor Stephen Wood. Please visit www.le.ac.uk for further information.

Not lovin' it: how insecure work creates insecure lifestyles for the poorest in society

***An article from** The Conversation.*

THE CONVERSATION

Pete Robertson, Associate Professor, Edinburgh Napier University

The claim that Eskimos have 50 words for snow may be apocryphal, but it neatly illustrates the truism that our vocabulary becomes more extensive and nuanced for phenomena we encounter frequently.

The bog-standard job of the 20th century was formal, full-time and permanent. Recently the lexicon for other kinds of jobs has expanded. Work can be temporary, fixed-term, seasonal, project-based, part-time, on a zero-hours contract, casual, agency, freelance, peripheral, contingent, external, non-standard, atypical, platform-based, outsourced, sub-contracted, informal, undeclared, insecure, marginal or precarious.

"Self-entrepreneurs" now do "Uber-jobs" – a term that arose (mimicking the earlier pejorative term "McJobs" for low pay/quality work) to describe the use of workers who are technically self-employed in the gig economy. The atypical job is no longer quite so atypical. Insecure work has become an important phenomenon.

Employment is a field where predictions of the future have been reliable, because the trends have been clear for some time now that growth in insecure employment has reached a point to become a subject of study. In the 1990s, management guru Charles Handy talked about the organisation of the future having a clover leaf design, with three kinds of human resource: full-time employees, casual staff and outsourced workers.

This threefold division was echoed in economist Will Hutton's darker prediction of a society in which 30% of people were disadvantaged and marginalised, 30% led insecure lives and 40% were privileged.

Visions of 21st-century careers

Careers at the start of the 21st century, we were told, would become "boundaryless" (hopping from project to project, not limited to one organisation), "portfolio" (multiple parallel jobs with multiple employers), and "protean" (with shapeshifting workers reinventing themselves as required).

Careers experts began to argue that the workers of the future needed to be ultra-flexible. Say goodbye to the job for life. Learn career management skills to dance nimbly to the tune of the new labour market. But this prescribed wisdom is problematic for four reasons.

First, job insecurity has always existed; it was once the historical norm. The construction industry has always been project-based and seasonal like agriculture; seafarers were traditionally hired for a voyage. The entertainment industry was literally the "gig economy". These are among the industries that routinely discarded workers when the job was done.

What is new is the extension of insecure work into industries where it was not previously common. This has been facilitated by new technology and the widespread use of contractual arrangements that seek to limit workers' rights.

Second, the vision of a brave new world of portfolio, boundaryless and protean careers was intended for professionals who could sell high-value parcels of work. It suits those with enough economic confidence to fly without the safety net of a regular income. These ideas were not dreamed up for the bicycle courier, the taxi driver or the peripatetic care worker, and certainly not for those trapped in a low-pay, no-pay cycle.

Third, the career management rhetoric lost sight of the distinction between is and should. Growth in atypical working patterns does not imply a moral imperative that workers should facilitate this development by shaping themselves into the desired mould. Particularly where some employers might be seeking to off-load responsibility for sick pay, holiday pay and travel between jobs.

Flexibility in human resources allows employers to scale operations up and down rapidly, and with minimal cost. This is not just about keeping wage bills down, but also about employers reducing levels of economic risk, while workers increase their share of risk bearing. The challenge of global competition may be inevitable, but an unquestioning compliance with employer regimes for sharing wealth and risk is not.

Finally, new technology facilitates rapid allocation of work tasks. At the same time it can dismantle jobs into discrete micro-tasks for which labour can be bought and sold remotely. In doing so it may have the side effect of de-personalising the relationship between worker and supervisor and removing workers from social interaction with their fellow staff. A lifestyle of isolated and isolating tasks makes it harder to forge a strong sense of social identity.

Insecurity in the UK

The Taylor Review of Modern Working Practices is intended to signal that the UK Government has woken up and smelled the coffee. It advocates the introduction of a new "dependent contractor" status for workers, but for the most part its recommendations are timid. Recently, the gig economy's biggest fish, Uber and Deliveroo, were taken to task by MPs. But so far it has been in employment law disputes, and not in Whitehall, that things have moved on.

Insecure workers may have to adapt. But they can resist too, although it is not easy. They are not well placed to afford trades union membership; being troublesome can lead to reduced work offers, and their identification with a trade may be limited. Nonetheless in the early skirmishes of what is likely to be a long-running social conflict it is the unions that have emerged with initial success.

The latest example is McDonald's, where staff at two fast-food outlets have just taken the unusual step of striking to demand better pay, more secure contracts and union recognition.

This is not just an issue of workers' rights. When people become locked into long-term lifestyles of insecure work, it interacts with other issues. With the high cost of housing, it traps individuals in a life cycle limbo of dependency on parents. There are reasons to believe that poor quality jobs with insecure work patterns have harmful effects on health. These detriments fall disproportionately on those in the least prosperous socioeconomic groups.

As for the way we educate young people about careers, exhortations to flexibility are good only up to a point. We need to equip workers of the future to collaborate to promote and safeguard their interests, and give them a fair chance to redress the power imbalance in contemporary labour markets.

8 September 2017

⇨ The above information is reprinted with kind permission from *The Conversation*. Please visit www.theconversation.com for further information.

Taking control of your work–life balance

By Sarah Deedat

Today marks the start of National Work Life Week. Work–life balance is a term you'll probably be familiar with – particularly if you have a job that makes significant demands on your time. But could you pin down what it actually is? And how would you know if you've achieved it?

If you're not sure, you're not alone! Experts across a range of social sciences have looked into aspects of work–life balance, but there's no agreed definition of the concept as a whole. Initially the idea was focused on women in the workplace, and the balance between their job and family responsibilities. The discussion has widened since then, and the concept of work-life balance continues to evolve over time, as social and technological factors around employment change.

It may also look different across borders. For example, consider that the average person in Turkey works 20 hours more per week than the average person in The Netherlands. This goes to show just how different one person's concept of work–life balance might be from someone else's.

Work–life balance in the modern world

Technology has been a great driver of efficiency in modern work. But it also enables an 'always on' work culture, where many employees can be productive outside the work environment. They can also make contact (and be contacted!) anywhere and everywhere. This disrupts the boundary between work life and non-work life, which can make achieving work–life balance more of a challenge.

Why is work–life balance important?

While the picture of a 'perfect' work–life balance might not be clear, we do know the benefits of getting it right. If you look after yourself well and achieve a good balance, you'll be a more productive worker and less likely to experience burnout. It will also improve things outside of work, like relationships.

We also know that an imbalance between work life and home life has implications for your physical and mental health. Someone with poor work–life balance will be at increased risk of:

⇨ high blood pressure and heart rate, and increased levels of the hormone cortisol – changes that happen as a result of increased stress

⇨ drinking too much alcohol

⇨ depression.

Someone with poor work–life balance is also more likely to have a negative perception of their own health, which can have an adverse impact on health in the long run.

So it's not just a 'nice-to-have'; it's a crucial factor in protecting our health and well-being.

Do I have a good work–life balance?

Although we might not have a universal definition of work–life balance, there are some questions you can ask yourself that may help you build a picture of your situation. One research-based model of work–life balance suggests it's made up of three 'domains'. I've outlined them here, with a couple of questions for you to think about for each one.

Work interference with personal life

⇨ Do you put your personal life on hold for work?

⇨ Are you unhappy with the amount of time you have for non-work activities?

Personal life interference with work

⇨ Does your personal life drain you of energy for work?

⇨ Is it hard to work because of personal matters?

Work/personal life enhancement

⇨ Does your personal life give you energy for your job?

⇨ Do you have a better mood because of your job?

How can I improve my work–life balance?

Unfortunately there's no miracle cure or step-by-step guide to achieving that elusive work–life balance. But a goal-centred approach may help you to work towards a better balance.

Start with a small, achievable goal or adjustment – one that's too easy to put off. It could be as simple as committing to leaving work on time once a week. Or you could decide on a time you'll stop checking your emails in the evening, and stick to it. Whatever your goal is, make sure it's specific: where and when will you do it? And how long for?

Once you've achieved that behavioural goal and embedded it into your routine, move on to the next. Through small, manageable goals you'll gradually gain more control over the behaviours that are disrupting the work–life balance you desire.

Of course there may be factors that make it very difficult to make even these small changes. If you're consistently overloaded with work or your employer has unrealistic expectations of you, it will be harder to set this process in motion. If this is the case, you'll need to have an honest conversation with your manager, or speak to your HR department. Remember your employer has a legal duty to reduce work-related stress and prevent it affecting your health.

But as much as you can, try and play an active role in shaping your own habits. One step at a time, using a goal-centred approach, you can take control of your work–life balance and improve your overall well-being.

2 October 2017

⇨ The above information is reprinted with kind permission from Bupa. Please visit www.bupa.co.uk for further information.

Without equality of income there can be no equality of opportunity

An article from **The Conversation.**

THE CONVERSATION

Kate Pickett, Professor of Epidemiology, University of York and Richard Wilkinson, Honorary Visiting Professor of Social Epidemiology, University of York

If moving forward is the goal, it's not a good policy to stand still. Yet we hear little from the Government about solutions to Britain's poor record on social mobility. Earlier this year both the current administration and its predecessors were roundly condemned for their failure to make any headway.

Research has repeatedly shown the clear link between high levels of income inequality and low levels of social mobility.

British social mobility is damaged by the UK's high income inequality. Economists have argued that young people from low-income families are less likely to invest in their own human capital development (their education) in more unequal societies. Young people are more likely to drop out of high school in more unequal US states or to be NEET (Not in Education, Employment or Training) in more unequal rich countries. Average educational performance on maths and literacy tests is lower in more unequal countries.

It isn't that young people in unequal societies lack aspirations. In fact, they are more likely to aspire to success. The sad thing is they are less likely to achieve it.

But the ways in which inequality hampers social mobility go far beyond educational involvement and attainment. In unequal societies, more parents will have mental illness or problems with drugs and alcohol. They will be more likely to be burdened by debt and long working hours, adding stress to family life. More young women will have babies as teenagers, more young men will be involved in violence.

Yet if we really tackle inequality, we can expect not only improvements in social mobility but in many other problems at the same time. It's not enough to focus on educational fixes for social immobility, nor even on poverty reduction and raising the minimum wage. We need to tackle inequality itself, and that includes changing the culture of runaway salaries and bonuses at the top of the income distribution.

For a long time this has felt like an insurmountable challenge, but reducing inequality within and between all countries is now one of the 17 United Nations Sustainable Development Goals (SDGs), to which the UK is a signatory.

There are targets and indicators to monitor progress on reducing inequality and they should be held government accountable for this. Unicef recently reported that the UK ranks 13th among rich countries in meeting the SDGs for children. But it ranked 34th on the hunger goal, and 31st on decent work and economic growth.

As the fifth biggest economy in the world (based on GDP per capita), Britain should be doing better for all its children and young people.

The June report by the Social Mobility Commission concluded that most public policy to improve social mobility under prime ministers Tony Blair, Gordon Brown, David Cameron and Theresa May either failed to improve the situation – or demonstrably made things worse.

Suggested improvements included cross departmental government strategy, ten-year targets for long term change, and a social mobility 'test' for all new relevant public policy. It also recommended that public spending be redistributed to address geographical, wealth and generational inequalities. And it advised government coalitions with local councils, communities and employers to create a national effort to improve social mobility.

So far as they go, applying these 'lessons' could indeed be helpful. But specific policy recommendations to address social mobility will not reduce the income and wealth inequalities which are at its root.

Appetite for change

So, is there a mandate for change? On the same day as the depressing news about a lack of progress on social mobility, the British Social Attitudes Survey released its annual findings. The results suggested that the public are in favour of progressive change. As many as 48% of people surveyed support higher tax and more public spending, up from 32% at the start of austerity in 2010.

Support for spending on benefits for disabled people is up to 67%, compared with 53% in 2010. And the proportion of people believing benefits claimants were 'fiddling' the system dropped to 22% – the lowest level in 30 years. The proportion of the population who thought that government should redistribute income from rich to poor was up to 42%, compared to 28% who disagreed. This is a strong mandate for reducing income inequality and ending austerity.

The evidence which shows the damage caused by socioeconomic inequality is mounting. The UK government risks being on the wrong side of history if it continues to fail to address the divide – and condemn us all to its devastating impact.

14 August 2017

⇨ The above information is reprinted with kind permission from *The Conversation*. Please visit www.theconversation.com for further information.

Youth jobs index

An extract from the August 2017 report on NEET.

Since 2012, the Government has reported a steady decline in the number of 16–24-year-olds who spend time not in education, employment or training (NEET).

This is good news, but it only tells half the story. There are still hundreds of thousands of young people spending very long periods of time NEET. Spending six months or more NEET has a long wage-scarring effect.

The Youth Jobs Index is designed to better understand this issue. It pools data points to understand:

⇨ the characteristics of young people spending time NEET

⇨ how many, and which, young people spend long amounts of time NEET

⇨ how well are young people sustaining their exits from being NEET.

1. Progress on the numbers of long-term NEET has stalled

The headline NEET figures are falling. The last ONS publication, covering January to March 2017, reported that 800,000 (11.2%) young people were presently NEET – a 68,000 reduction on the same quarter in 2016.

This fall is welcome, as is the longer-term fall from the peak quarterly figure of 1,163,000 in 2011. However, this snapshot figure fails to show something important – how long young people are spending NEET. A short time out of education or work might be expected at the transition to adulthood, but a long period has damaging long-term effects. Our analysis shows that many young people experience long periods NEET that cannot easily be seen from the quarterly figures.

Nearly two million young people between 16 and 24 spend some time NEET. As the table below shows, of this two million the majority (1.18 million) spend more than six months NEET. A very significant proportion, 811,000, or one in ten of all young people, spend a year or more out of education or work. This is an increase on the figures in last year's report which showed 714,000 spending 12 months or more NEET.

Worryingly, the most recent Department for Education quarterly figures, published in May 2017, and which could not be included in our full analysis, revealed a statistically significant rise in the number of young people 16 to 18 NEET in England.

Since the introduction of the Raised Participation Age (RPA) in England in 2014, all young people should be in some form of education or work-based training until they are 18. The RPA policy means that in effect, the NEET rate for 16- to 18-year-olds should be zero. Instead, there are 134,000 people in this age group, who are not in education, training or work at all.

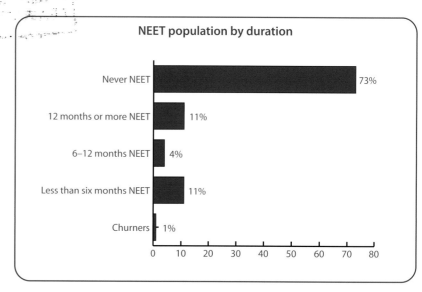

NEET population by duration

Category	Percentage
Never NEET	73%
12 months or more NEET	11%
6–12 months NEET	4%
Less than six months NEET	11%
Churners	1%

2. Qualifications matter

The impact of qualifications on NEET status

Young people in the UK are increasingly well-qualified – 79% to Level 2 or above, and nearly 40% to Level 3 or above. Given this, it's not surprising that if we look at all the young people spending any time NEET, the majority have a Level 2 qualification or higher.

But the fact that qualifications count can clearly be seen when we look at who spends long periods of time NEET.

Proportionately, more young people with no (or below) Level 2 qualifications are likely to spend six months or more NEET.

As a result, they make up a disproportionate part of the long-term NEET population.

As we can see in the two charts below, young people with above Level 2 qualifications represent over half of young people who are NEET for more than six months. But when we look at young people who are NEET for 12 months or longer, we can see that those with qualifications at Level 2 or below make up a clear majority. Having a qualification above Level 2 certainly seems to help young people avoid long-term NEET status.

We can look at the role qualifications play in a different way by looking at how they affect a young person's risk of being NEET. The risk of being NEET for six months or more varies strongly with qualifications. Failure to achieve a Level 2 qualification means you are twice as likely to be long-term NEET.

For those with higher level qualifications (Level 3, Level 4 and above), whilst 10% are at risk of spending six months or more NEET, only 3% are at risk of being NEET for 12 months or longer.

Our analysis shows that Level 2 qualifications do provide some protection against spending long periods NEET.

But those who go on to college and university are even less likely to be long-term NEET and therefore more immune from the associated scarring effect.

> **"I received no feedback. I tried phoning and emailing and then recently I saw on a government website that the vacancy had been filled. I need to know if there are areas where I need to improve my skills. Just a simple email saying the vacancy has gone to somebody else would help. I keep going because I want a career in IT. I worked for my qualification. My mum and dad understand I want to work in IT. They say that I shouldn't just go and work in Tesco."**
>
> **Young male learner, 21, Adviza**

3. Women stay inactive, men 'churn' in and out

'Unemployed' vs 'inactive'

The NEET population is officially classified into two different groups; those who are 'unemployed' and those who are 'economically inactive'. 'Unemployed' refers to an individual who is out of work, but looking for and able to work immediately. The latter describes individuals who are not looking for and not available to start work immediately.

The January to March 2017 ONS snapshot suggests that of the 800,000 16–24-year-olds who were NEET in that quarter, 334,000 (42%) were unemployed and 466,000 (58%) were economically inactive.

There is a gender split. Women are more likely to be economically inactive (66% of this group are female) while men are more likely to be unemployed (60% of this group are male).

According to research by the Young Women's Trust, 61% of economically inactive young women said they were not seeking work because they were caring for their family and homes. While many want to work, in most cases when interviewed, low wages, poor work-related support and job insecurity were cited as the main reasons for inactivity.

What happens after the 'snapshot'

This context is important when looking at what happens to young

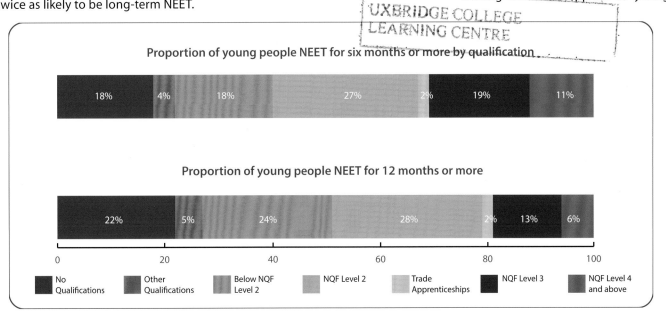

Proportion of young people NEET for six months or more by qualification

| 18% | 4% | 18% | 27% | 2% | 19% | 11% |

Proportion of young people NEET for 12 months or more

| 22% | 5% | 24% | 28% | 2% | 13% | 6% |

0   20   40   60   80   100

- ■ No Qualifications
- Other Qualifications
- Below NQF Level 2
- NQF Level 2
- Trade Apprenticeships
- ■ NQF Level 3
- NQF Level 4 and above

people NEET over the course of a year. In other words, the quarterly figures give us a snapshot – but what happens to the young people in the picture afterwards, and does this change depend on whether they are inactive or unemployed? Or whether they are men or women?

Young people defined as unemployed and therefore available to work, are much more likely to enter work (or sometimes education) over the course of a year, but also much more likely to fall out of work and back into being NEET again. 47% of unemployed young people who start the year NEET will finish the year still NEET, although they are likely to have been in work at some points during the year. 33% of unemployed young people stay NEET for the entire year.

The picture for economically inactive young people is different. Over half (52%) of young people who are economically inactive spend a year or more NEET, compared to 33% of unemployed young people. Meaning, perhaps unsurprisingly, economically inactive young people are not experiencing the same levels of churn as their unemployed peers.

We know that males who are NEET are more likely to be unemployed while females who are NEET are more likely to be economically inactive. This distinction has little impact on the proportion of men (43%) and women (44%) spending the entire year NEET. Of interest is that while more women are inactive compared to men, they are slightly better at finding a job and keeping it for six months compared to men.

The variances between NEET populations indicate that the groups require tailored responses. The greater levels of churn experienced by unemployed young people, who tend to be men, suggest that they chiefly need support to stay in work, once they have found a job.

Whereas the majority of economically inactive young people, who are mainly women, spend 12 months or more NEET, which suggests they require more support to overcome barriers to employment, become work ready, and enter a job.

August 2017

⇨ The above information is reprinted with kind permission from Impetus. Please visit www.impetus-pef.org.uk for further information.

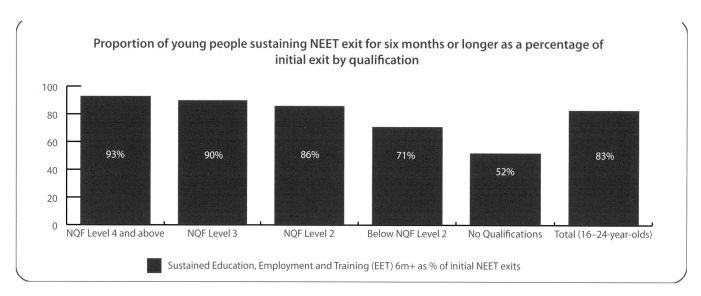

Proportion of young people sustaining NEET exit for six months or longer as a percentage of initial exit by qualification

- Sustained Education, Employment and Training (EET) 6m+ as % of initial NEET exits

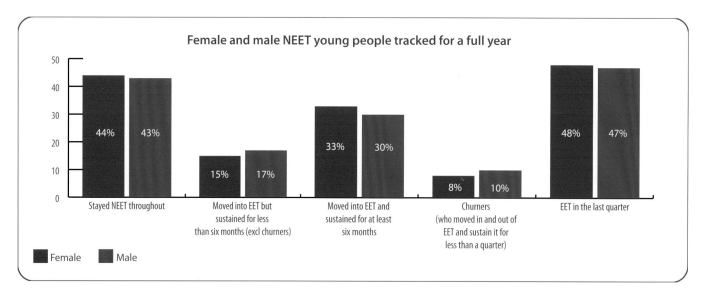

Female and male NEET young people tracked for a full year

Youth unemployment

As with adult unemployment, the level of unemployment of 16–24-year-olds peaked in the UK during 2011, when it reached over one million (a rate of 22%) and continued to fall as the economy started to grow. By the end of 2014 youth unemployment fell to around 840,000 – at a rate of 18%. The downward trend continued and by September 2017 it was down to just 10.3%. However, 16–24-year-olds remain the highest group at risk of unemployment, with 35–49-year-olds being the least at risk, with a rate of just 2.8% in the year to October 2017.

Despite the downward trend, observers in the UK and around the world – from the UK's National Institute of Economic and Social Research to the World Economic Forum – agree that youth unemployment represents one of the most serious economic and social problems facing developed and developing economies alike.

According to the ILO, in 2013, as least 73 million 16- to 24-year-olds were unemployed, representing 12.6% of all active 16–24-year-olds. In terms of world regions, North African youth unemployment is the highest, at 27.9%, with the Middle East at 26.5%. In some countries in the Arab world, up to 90% of 16–24-year-olds are unemployed. Youth unemployment in the EU as a whole stands at 21.4%, but there is considerable variation. Greece now tops the pile, with a youth unemployment rate of over 59% – nearly three times the EU average, while in Germany the rate is 7.5% – just one third of the EU average. In fact, in Germany there were 30,000 unfilled vacancies in training programmes for young workers.

In the UK there are around 7.3 million young people aged between 16 and 24 – roughly two-thirds (4.8 million) are 'economically active' and one-third are 'economically inactive'. The economically active are either working or available for and seeking work, i.e. employed or unemployed, and the economically inactive are not available or not seeking work. Most of these (1.8 million) are students.

So what lies behind embedded youth unemployment? According to the World Economic Forum, the main causes of youth unemployment include:

1. A lack of quality of education and relevance to the needs of the labour market.

2. Economic downturns – which historically increase youth unemployment – and where young workers are often seen as the most dispensable; population growth, especially in North Africa and the Middle East.

3. 'Discouraged youth' where many young workers have given up hope of ever acquiring a meaningful job which provides a 'living wage'. As the OECD also puts it, the 16–24-year-olds also face very specific barriers into the labour market, and where there is weak integration of young workers, given the mismatch that exists between the current demand for labour, and the effective supply of young workers – in short, many young workers are neither willing nor able to accept the kind of jobs that are available.

Youth unemployment in the UK has risen consistently during the last three recessions – in 1993 it was 15%, and by 2008 it has risen to 19%, peaking at 22% in 2011 for 16–24-year-olds, and at 20% for the 18- to 24-year-olds.

According to the Commission on Youth Unemployment, unemployed young people represents a financial time-bomb, with an estimated direct cost to the exchequer (in 2012) of £4.8 billion (more than the budget for further education for 16- to 19-year-olds in England) and indirect cost to the economy of £10.7 billion in lost output.

Of special concern is the number of long-term unemployed young people – defined as looking for work for 12 months or more – and NEETS. NEETS include those 16–24-year-olds who are unemployed or economically inactive and not in any form of education, employment or training.

As in the 1980s and 90s, recent government policy has focused on supply-side incentives, including the introduction of a Youth Contract, which includes an injection of £1 bilion to get young unemployed people working or studying – the 'earning or learning' initiative. It includes wage incentives worth more than £2,275 for each 18–24-year-old an employer recruits or provides with work experience placements. There are also incentive payments to support employers to create apprenticeships and £126 million to help teenagers into education, employment or training. Doubts clearly remain regarding the extent to which such modest government initiatives can really 'change the game'. It is clearly time to put vocational education back on the front-burner while taking a closer look at Germany, Austria and Finland – where youth unemployment is simply not an issue.

⇨ The above information is reprinted with kind permission from Economics Online. Please visit www.economicsonline.co.uk for further information.

© 2018 Economics Online

How young people can solve the youth employment crisis

Unemployment, and crucially, underemployment, is a challenge faced by young people around the world.

By Jenny Bowie

With young people four times more likely to be out of work, it is hard to deny that we have a youth employment crisis. This is despite decades of employment programmes and initiatives targeting young people. Urgent solutions are needed to meet the challenge to create the estimated 600 million new jobs that will be needed by 2030.

Last year, as part of Restless Development's work with the Solutions for Youth Employment (S4YE) coalition, I travelled to India and Colombia to hear from young people their ideas for how to solve this crisis, and what their role should be in leading the response.

In Colombia I met Lina, a 26-year-old marketing intern living in Bogotá, who shared her passion for changing attitudes of employers towards young people.

She said: "As millennials we present magnificent qualities that have not been explored by many, mainly for fear of difference and the unknown.

We are young people full of energy, with desire to learn and contribute. We are active, creative, and eager to eat the world, but many have closed their doors."

Young people in Colombia also highlighted the inequalities faced by young people outside the capital. Julio from Sandonar, near the Ecuador border, encourages young people to create their own jobs by taking up much forgotten traditional handicrafts.

He added: "We see entrepreneurship as an opportunity to improve the quality of life for us and our families, of course with a vision of building a country. However, the lack of technical and economic resources limits the progress of our projects."

On the other side of the world, Sunidhi, a 24-year-old co-founder of Reaching Sky Foundation, working in the Delhi slums, believes young people, quality education and empowerment are the solutions to avoid stagnation in the job market.

She said: "Youth issues are many but the source is one. It is challenging but it is not impossible to turn our wishful thinking into reality. We have created our challenges and we are the only solution. We need to conquer our fear and have faith in our dream of a better us, and better world, by keeping our big hopes and big actions stronger."

In India I also met Alex, a 22-year-old student from Tamil Nadu who founded a youth movement to create awareness of self-sufficiency and established a community shop selling produce made by young people.

He said: "The youth need to be enabled to become job generators then job seekers. I believe that a sustainable livelihood can achieve the economic development and it helps to attain the national development."

These are only four examples of young people taking action to tackle youth unemployment in their communities; however, they demonstrate that young people have many of the solutions that the public, private and third sector are looking for, and young people have the initiative and drive to take these forward.

Crucially, young people I spoke with, want to lead these solutions, by meaningfully working alongside governments, employers and civil society, to ensure all young people, in every country, can access decent and productive work.

23 February 2018

⇨ The above information is reprinted with kind permission from Restless Development. Please visit www.wearerestless.org for further information.

Internships cost job seekers £1,000 a month in London and £827 in Manchester

Internships are "shutting" disadvantaged people out of careers.

By Steven Hopkins

The cost of undertaking an unpaid internship to land a job in "desirable sectors" will now set a jobseeker back £1,019 a month in London and £827 in Manchester.

According to The Sutton Trust, people from low and moderate-income backgrounds are being prevented from accessing internships – which are "increasingly seen as a requirement before a first job" due to rising rents in the two centres and inflation.

Separately, research carried out for the Trade Union Congress found that 78% of 18-34-year-olds could not afford to live in London away from home to become an unpaid intern.

The Trust said that 40% of young people who have carried out an internship have done at least one of them unpaid, leading to concerns that "the significant costs associated with unpaid internships are shutting many less advantaged young people out of careers".

A six-month internship in London, even if transport costs are provided, would leave a single person £6,114 out of pocket and in Manchester a young person would need £5,556 to get by, the Trust said.

The figures represent a 10% increase in the capital since 2014, when a six-month internship would cost a jobseeker £926 (£93 less) a month, or £5,556 (£558 less) over six months.

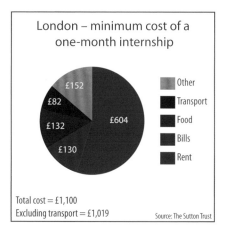

London – minimum cost of a one-month internship

£152 Other
£82 Transport
£132 Food
£130 Bills
£604 Rent

Total cost = £1,100
Excluding transport = £1,019

Source: The Sutton Trust

In Manchester costs increased by £39 a month, or £234 over six months, during the same period – an increase of just under 5%.

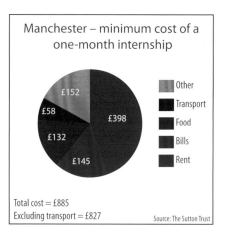

Manchester – minimum cost of a one-month internship

£152 Other
£58 Transport
£132 Food
£145 Bills
£398 Rent

Total cost = £885
Excluding transport = £827

Source: The Sutton Trust

The Trust is calling for all internships over four weeks (£4,976 in London, £3,308 in Manchester) to be paying at least the minimum wage of £7.50 per hour and "ideally" the Living Wage of £8.56 (£10.20 in London).

It also recommends that internships are advertised publicly and that recruitment processes are "fair, transparent and based on merit".

"Failure to do so prevents young people from low and moderate-income backgrounds from accessing jobs in some of the most desirable sectors such as journalism, fashion, the arts and politics," the Trust report – *Internships – unpaid, unadvertised, unfair* – states.

The Trust cited the recent Taylor review, which examined modern working practices, in its report. The review concluded that "it is clear to us that unpaid internships are an abuse of power by employers and extremely damaging to social mobility".

Minimum wage legislation makes many unpaid internships illegal "but the law is not properly enforced", the Trust said, citing, as evidence, the fact the Government recently confirmed that there have been no recorded prosecutions in relation to interns and the National Minimum Wage.

Key points:

⇨ Organisations continue to offer internships which are unpaid, and offer internships without formally advertising them.

⇨ An internship would cost a single person £1,019 a month in London and £827 in Manchester.

⇨ Over 40% of young people who have carried out an internship have done at least one of them unpaid.

⇨ There are 70,000 interns in the UK at any one time.

⇨ Roughly 10,000 graduates are carrying out an internship at six months post-graduation, with 20% of them doing so unpaid.

⇨ There are concerns that some employers are either unaware that their interns should be paid, or that some employers are exploiting the lack of clarity in the law to avoid paying their interns.

The Sutton Trust said that since 2014, there has been "some moves in the right direction" by employers, such as Pret a Manger, who started paying their interns. The Brit Awards also introduced ten paid internships to help "open up access to the music industry", it said, and there are reports that publishing houses are increasingly introducing paid internships.

However, the Trust lamented that organisations were continuing to advertise for unpaid interns online and through 'informal networks'.

Examples of internships advertised this month which the Trust highlighted include – a major fashion designer who was looking for an unpaid design intern to work for two-to-three months in the lead-up to their London Fashion

Week show and an MP who advertised a six-month internship with "no set hours and only expenses covered".

The role involved undertaking research, analysis and briefings on upcoming issues, the Trust said. It declined to name the MP.

"Given that MPs are already considerably more likely to be from a privileged background than the constituents that they represent, it is extremely disappointing that MPs continue to offer unpaid internships, locking less well-off young people out of politics," the report reads.

"Additionally, concerns have also been raised by the APPG on Social Mobility that internships in politics are often given out to family and friends of politicians, rather than being openly advertised."

In the UK there are around 70,000 internships each year and research by the Trust shows that 10,000 graduates are in unpaid internships six months after graduation, "though many more will do them at other times".

There are no official figures on the number of interns in the UK, but IPPR analysis has found that around 11,000 internships per year are formally advertised online and an annual survey by the Department for Education found that 6% of businesses surveyed providing some form of paid or unpaid internship.

However, the graduate careers guidance service Prospects carried out an online survey of almost 9,000 16–25-year-olds in 2017 and found that 48% had undertaken an unpaid internship.

The Trust is backing a bill by Conservative peer Lord Holmes of Richmond "tightening" minimum wage legislation to ban unpaid internships over four weeks long. The bill is also been supported by the All-Party Parliamentary Group on Social Mobility and the Government's Social Mobility Commission, the Trust noted.

Sir Peter Lampl, Founder and Chairman of The Sutton Trust and Chairman of the Education Endowment Foundation, said: "Around 40% of young people who have carried out an internship have done so unpaid. All internships over four weeks should

be paid at least the minimum wage of £7.50 per hour. Failure to do so prevents young people from low and moderate-income backgrounds from accessing jobs in some of the most desirable sectors such as journalism, fashion, the arts and politics.

"All internship positions should be advertised publicly. Large numbers of internships are never advertised and instead offered through informal networks. This practice locks out young people without connections. Also, the process by which potential candidates are selected for internships should uphold the same standards of recruitment as for other jobs."

Unpaid internships, the Trust said, are a "particular problem" in sought-after professions such as the arts and media, where the Social Mobility Commission has reported a dramatic rise in the number of unpaid internships.

Sharon White, CEO of the broadcasting regulator Ofcom, recently called on TV executives to stop using unpaid internships, due to concerns that they are limiting access to the industry.

While the Trust said "the best unpaid internships can kick-start a career, there is evidence that undertaking an unpaid internship can actually reduce future earnings". Recent work from the Institute for Social and Economic Research, it said, found that three years after graduating, former unpaid interns earned less than those who went immediately into paid work or further study.

What can unpaid interns do to challenge their pay?

The Sutton Trust says:

"An unpaid intern can report an organisation to the Government's Pay and Work Rights Helpline, or can take a case to a tribunal. However, this is a potentially difficult process for an intern who is relying on their placement to help them break into an industry, and risks them losing access to the references and contacts that they have worked unpaid to build.

"Additionally, even if an intern does take a case to a tribunal, under the current law an employer often can still claim that the intern was under no obligation to attend work, or had no obligation to

give notice that they would no longer attend – making them unentitled to the minimum wage."

The Sutton Trust's recommendations:

1. **All internships longer than one month should be paid at least the National Minimum Wage**

To open up access to internship opportunities, interns should be paid at least the National Minimum Wage (£7.05 per hour for 21-24-year-olds, or £7.50 for over-25s). Preferably, interns should be paid the Living Wage of £8.75 (or London Living Wage, £10.20, in London). The current law should be tightened to ban unpaid internships over four weeks in length.

2. **Internship positions should be advertised publicly, rather than being filled informally**

Large numbers of internships are never advertised, and instead offered through informal networks, for example to friends or family of staff. This practice locks out talented young people without connections, limiting their opportunities and hampering their social mobility. All internships should be advertised publicly, so that regardless of connections, all potential applicants can apply.

3. **Recruitment processes should be fair, transparent and based on merit**

As well as being openly advertised, the process by which potential candidates are selected for internships should be fair and transparent – upholding the same standards of recruitment as other jobs. All internships should be awarded on merit to the best candidate, not based on personal connections.

30 January 2018

⇨ The above information is reprinted with kind permission from The Huffington Post UK. Please visit www.huffingtonpost.co.uk for further information.

What is an apprenticeship?

In 2016/17, 92% of apprentices said their career prospects had improved as a result of completing an apprenticeship – find out everything you need to know about joining them on this popular career path.

How apprenticeships work

Apprenticeships allow you to combine work and study by mixing on-the-job training with classroom learning. You'll be employed to do a real job while studying for a formal qualification, usually for one day a week either at a college or a training centre. By the end of your apprenticeship, you'll hopefully have gained the skills and knowledge needed to either succeed in your chosen career or progress onto the next apprenticeship level.

What you'll learn depends on the role that you're training for. However, apprentices in every role follow an approved study programme, which means you'll gain a nationally-recognised qualification at the end of your apprenticeship.

These qualifications can include:

⇨ **Functional skills** – GCSE level qualifications in English, maths and IT.

⇨ **National Vocational Qualifications** (NVQs) – from level 2 (comparable to five GCSEs) up to level 5 (similar to a postgraduate degree).

⇨ **Technical certificates** – such as BTEC, City and Guild Progression Award, etc.

⇨ **Academic qualifications** – including a Higher National Certificate (HNC), Higher National Diploma (HND), foundation degree or the equivalent of a full Bachelors degree.

You'll also be constantly developing your transferable skills, otherwise known as soft skills, which are highly valued by employers. These include communication, teamwork and problem solving, as well as knowledge of IT and the application of numbers.

Apprenticeship levels

There are four different levels of apprenticeship:

⇨ **Intermediate** – equivalent to five good GCSE passes.

⇨ **Advanced** – equivalent to two A-level passes.

⇨ **Higher** – equivalent to the first stages of higher education, such as a foundation degree.

⇨ **Degree** – comparable to a Bachelors or Masters degree.

⇨ Apprenticeship-level structures vary across different countries in the UK.

Types of apprenticeships

Most job sectors offer apprenticeship opportunities in the UK, with a wide range of specific roles on offer within each. These include:

⇨ Business apprenticeships in roles such as accounting, digital marketing, people/HR administration, recruitment and sales.

⇨ Construction apprenticeships in roles such as building, plumbing and quantity surveying.

⇨ Engineering apprenticeships in roles such as civil engineering, mechanical engineering and electrical engineering.

⇨ Healthcare apprenticeships in roles such as dental, nursing and youth work, as well as NHS apprenticeships.

⇨ IT apprenticeships in roles such as information security and software development.

⇨ Law apprenticeships offered at paralegal, legal executive or solicitor level.

⇨ Media apprenticeships in roles such as journalism, live events and costume design.

You'll be able to enter your chosen sector at an apprenticeship level that reflects your previous qualifications and the demands of the role.

Length of apprenticeships

The length of your apprenticeship will depend on a number of factors, such as the level of the apprenticeship, your chosen sector, employer requirements and your individual ability.

That being said, apprenticeships will usually last between one and six years. Their length follows a basic framework:

⇨ **intermediate apprenticeships** typically last between one year and 18 months

⇨ **advanced apprenticeships** are usually studied over two years

⇨ **higher and degree apprenticeships** take three-to-six years to complete.

It's worth checking directly with your chosen employer before applying to check how long your course will last, as some won't follow this structure.

Pay rates and working hours

As an apprentice, you're entitled to the National Minimum Wage, which currently stands at £3.50 per hour. This applies to all apprentices aged 16–18, or those in the first year of their course. Once you've progressed past this level, you'll be entitled to the minimum wage rate for your age.

This pay rate is stated as a guideline – some employers will pay you a higher wage. You'll also be entitled to sick pay, any additional benefits your employer offers to its other employees, such as healthcare plans and childcare vouchers, and at least 20 days of paid holiday per year.

Your working hours will vary depending on your employer, but you won't be able to work more than 40 hours per week or any fewer than 30. Typically, you'll work between 35 and 37.5 hours per week. The sector you're entering will determine the nature of your daily working hours – while most apprentices can expect to work a 9am–5.30pm day with an hour's break for lunch, those in hospitality or healthcare roles, for instance, should expect to work antisocial shifts.

Age limit

There is no upper age limit on being an apprentice. As long as you're over 16 and have the right credentials, you'll be eligible to apply for your chosen apprenticeship.

If you start your apprenticeship after you turn 19, you may be entitled to additional government funding – find out more about what's on offer at Student Finance England – Advanced Learner Loan.

Entry requirements

As each type of apprenticeship offers a different-levelled qualification on the Qualifications and Credit Framework (QCF), their entry requirements will vary. Generally speaking, they are as follows:

⇨ To apply for an **intermediate apprenticeship**, you'll just need to be over 16 years old and no longer in full-time education.

⇨ For an **advanced apprenticeship**, you're likely to be asked for prior work experience and at least three A*-C or 9-4 grade GCSEs or equivalent – such as an intermediate apprenticeship qualification.

⇨ As **higher apprenticeships** are the equivalent of a foundation degree, HNC or first year of a Bachelors, you'll usually need at least five A*-C or 9-4 grade GCSEs, as well as some Level 3 qualifications in relevant subjects, to apply. Your Level 3 qualifications could be AS-levels, a BTEC National or a level 3 NVQ.

⇨ **Degree apprenticeships** will have the tightest entry requirements. These may include three A-levels in a specified grade range or a higher apprenticeship qualification, on top of at least five A*-C or 9-4 GCSE grades. It's likely you'll be required to have prior work experience.

You can apply for apprenticeships at any time of the year – it all depends when an employer has a vacancy. You'll be able to check the specific entry requirements of your chosen apprenticeship once the position opens.

The difference between an apprenticeship and an internship

The terms 'apprenticeship' and 'internship' are sometimes mistakenly used interchangeably. To ensure you're applying for the right positions, it's important to understand the differences between these opportunities.

Apprenticeships are:

⇨ formal employment programmes and as such you'll sign a contract with your employer

⇨ long-term and take between one to four years to complete

⇨ more suited to those with a clear idea of what sector they'd like to work in and what career path they'd like to follow

⇨ commonly undertaken by school leavers

⇨ designed to provide specific work-based training. Apprentices learn by actually doing the job

⇨ a way for apprentices to gain formal qualifications such as NVQs, foundation degrees and technical certificates

⇨ paid, as at the very least you'll receive the National Minimum Wage

⇨ a direct route to employment, with the majority of apprentices guaranteed a job on completion of their programme.

Internships are:

⇨ informal arrangements as more often than not no employment contracts are signed

⇨ short-term, limited periods lasting between one week and 12 months

⇨ geared towards providing an insight to those who may be unsure of what career direction to take

⇨ typically undertaken by students and graduates

⇨ work-based learning opportunities, which focus more on supplying interns with transferable skills and experience for their CV rather than job-specific skills or formal qualifications

⇨ temporary, with no guarantee of employment on completion.

December 2017

⇨ The above information is reprinted with kind permission from Graduate Prospects Ltd. Please visit www.prospects.ac.uk for further information.

It's time to stop stigmatising apprenticeships as a second-class option

By Denise Hatton, Chief Executive of the National Council of YMCAs

Deciding what to do after leaving school can be a daunting task for many young people. Figuring out the rest of your life is never an easy decision but, for today's generation, it's probably harder than ever.

For most young people who are completing their GCSEs or A-Levels, university is often recognised as the 'main' option. But, with tuition fees now up to £9,000 per year and employers looking for practical experience as well as qualifications, young people are facing immense pressures.

To help young people gain the necessary skills and experience to enter the workplace, the Government is heavily promoting the vocational skills route, including apprenticeships. Part of this push is courtesy of the new Apprenticeship Levy that is being introduced to help fund three million new apprenticeship starts by 2020. There has been much debate about the Government's strategy on both sides of this argument and just last week, the Sub-Committee on Education, Skills and the Economy published a report criticising the levy, warning it'll be "doomed to fail" if the Government focuses on apprenticeship starts over quality.

While it's certain that the current apprenticeship offer will evolve once we've seen how the levy will play out in reality, many businesses have already realised the benefits of hiring apprentices. Yet young people's voices have been tragically absent from the ongoing apprenticeship debate so far.

That is where we believe YMCA's new Work in Progress research report, released today, will come in.

Over the past couple of months, we've been speaking to more than 400 young people who are either former or current apprentices. We've heard the positives and the negatives behind the vocational route into work and we've put forward in our report what we think needs to change to make apprenticeships work for more young people.

One of the starkest findings for us was around the perception of apprenticeships as second-class routes into work, with less than one in four of our respondents to our survey receiving any information about them from their teachers and lecturers.

Catherine, 18, from Swansea, told us: "In school, it was like you had to go to college and you had to go to university. Apprenticeships were seen for the people who didn't have brains to go do a degree. I don't think that's right, it's just a different skill."

However, the belief that apprenticeships are somewhat less worthy couldn't be further from the truth. Local YMCAs up and down in the country train almost 3,700 people through YMCA apprenticeships each year. In fact, by working with young people and businesses we know that apprenticeships are available in many different industries offering various levels of qualifications. And that's not all – almost 80% of the young people we spoke to were also offered a job at the end of their apprenticeship.

Listening to young people, it's evident that taking on an apprenticeship not only puts them on the path to employment, but takes away some of the anxieties they may face trying to get into work. Many employers recognise that would-be apprentices won't have the necessary work experience, giving young people the opportunity to gain first-hand experience on the job.

Carlie, 26, did an apprenticeship in administration and business and now works as a qualified youth worker. She told us: "When you start an apprenticeship, the expectation isn't there. They know and understand that you're training and that they're there to teach you. So you don't feel pressured to be perfect."

And that is just part of the reason why apprenticeships are such an important element of young people's routes into employment: they are an option. They provide those young people who are more practically minded, who want to pursue a career where university qualifications are less relevant or who simply learn in a different way a positive experience that helps get them into work.

Young people have told us what they need and it's time the sector listens. Only then can the apprenticeship offer improve and rightfully be seen as an attractive and progressive option that helps young people get their foot on the career ladder.

5 April 2017

⇨ The above information is reprinted with kind permission from YMCA. Please visit www.ymca.org.uk for further information.

Apprenticeships vs university

Deciding whether to study a professional qualification through an apprenticeship or to go to university can be a difficult choice.

Apprenticeships mean you can attain the same qualifications – without the degree – by starting on-the-job training from day one. University allows you to take your time choosing your next career move. We've outlined some considerations for both options below.

Arguments for apprenticeships

1. The qualifications are just as good

Former Skills minister Nick Boles advocated that apprenticeships should be considered a clear alternative to university.

"I would like to get to a place where there's a choice between two routes, both of which could take you as far as you want to go – one of which is a full-time university degree, the other is an apprenticeship," he said.

Take the AAT Advanced or Professional Apprenticeship in Accounting for example – apprentices are qualified to undertake a wide range of accountancy, financial and taxation tasks and have the opportunity to progress to chartered status, just like university graduates.

2. You'll earn more

There are strong financial reasons to consider apprenticeships, too. Research by the Centre for Economics and Business Research (CEBR) shows that those who progress on to study a Professional/Higher apprenticeship will increase earnings by an estimated £150,000 over a lifetime – with the bonus of no university debt.

You also earn a living while learning on the job. According to the National Apprenticeship Service, average pay rates for apprentices are around £170 per week.

Research also shows that the average university graduate has a starting salary of £14,734 while those who complete an apprenticeship on average have a starting salary of £18,463.

"We're not surprised at all that apprentices earn more within their first jobs than graduates, purely because they get the hands-on experience while they're learning," explains Spencer Mehlman, of notgoingtouni.co.uk.

"Their first job is typically within the company that they've trained with. Therefore they know everything already in terms of rules, what the company likes and dislikes and they have the experience with the customers and clients already."

3. It's real experience

Real-world experience is key, especially in accounting. A theoretical knowledge of accounting is not worth very much – what counts is how you can apply it to clients. Therefore, by having several years of experience under your belt by the time you finish your apprenticeship, you're a step ahead of those who have only studied accounting in books.

92% of apprentices feel their apprenticeship has positively improved their career prospects.

Arguments for university

1. Time to decide your future

Many young people interested in accounting will typically spend three years at university, followed by on-the-job training, followed by professional qualifications.

And for good reason. Just as university is not for everyone, neither are apprenticeships. If you don't have a clear idea of which career you want to enter, studying a traditional subject at university can help you to keep your career options open while gaining a qualification.

2. University life

There is also the issue of university life. Yes, there's the social side, and university also lets you experience full-time academic study for three years.

3. Degrees are still valued

While views are changing, there's still a sense that attending university helps get you ahead. In a recent poll, 56% of recent graduates felt that the biggest benefit of doing a degree was being "more qualified" than others when applying for a job.

⇨ The above information is reprinted with kind permission from The Association of Accounting Technicians. Please visit www.aat.org.uk for further information.

© 2018 The Association of Accounting Technicians

Apprenticeship vs Degree

Apprenticeship

£25.8k

Starting salary on completion of the National Grid's Advanced Apprenticeship Programme (careers.nationalgrid.com)

One in three

UK adults who believe apprenticeships offer better career prospects than degrees
(July 2014 poll by Sutton Trust and Pearson)

509,400

Apprenticeship starts in the 2015/16 academic year – up 56% since 2009/10
(Department for Business Innovation and Skills)

200,000

Apprenticeships that the Government have pledged to start by **2020**
(Department for Business Innovation and Skills)

25,000

Apprenticeship vacancies available online at any one time
(National Apprenticeship Service)

Degree

£18.6k–£22.8k

Starting salary range for UK degree graduates, according to a report from the Higher Education Careers Services Unit (What Do Graduates Do?)

One in ten

Recent graduates in the UK who are not currently employed, according to the Higher Education Standards Authority (HESA)

 **50%**

Recent graduates who are stuck in non-graduate level jobs, according to the Office for National Statistics

 **22%**

Graduates who achieved a first in 2014/15 (HESA)

 **11%**

Graduates who achieved a first in 2003 (HESA)

What are key skills? Employability skills to help you get a job

With so many young people out there looking for jobs, how do you stand out from the crowd and impress employers? This is where key skills come in.

Key skills are employability skills that you need for the world of work – and they're pretty important for life as well! By developing employability skills, you'll improve your chances of getting a job and thriving in your career.

But how do you gain these employability skills? Luckily, there are lots of different ways to develop them – including lessons or extracurricular activities at school, in a Saturday or holiday job, doing projects in your own time or work experience.

What are key skills?

Here is a list of key skills that employers typically look out for:

⇨ Communication

⇨ Teamwork

⇨ Initiative

⇨ Problem-solving

⇨ Computer / IT skills

⇨ Organisation

⇨ Leadership

⇨ Hard work and dedication

⇨ Creativity

⇨ Numeracy

⇨ Reliability.

How key skills or employability skills can boost your CV

According to jobs board Monster, employers consider key skills to be the most important section of your CV. A solid set of employability skills sets you apart from other applicants and shows the boss what you will bring to the job.

But it's important to bring this section to life rather than just writing a generic list of keys skills – you need to give specific examples. Don't worry if you've never had a job before – employability skills are transferable from school, clubs and other areas of life.

For example, instead of just having a bullet point saying you have "good communication skills", explain that you are a member of the debating team and have represented your school in public competitions.

Here are some of the top employability skills and ideas for how you can develop them (and then write about them on your CV).

Communication

Employers look for people who can speak and write clearly and accurately, so you'll need to prove that you have good oral and written skills. This is one of the most sought after employability skills according to a number of studies.

Good communication is vital in pretty much every job.

Verbal communication skills are particularly important for any job that involves working in a team or directly with people. Written skills are important for things like writing reports or dealing and negotiating with people over email.

It goes without saying that you should make sure your application is well written, without any typos or grammar gremlins. If you get this wrong, the recruiter might not even make it to the key skills section of your CV.

Practical examples you could give include a Saturday job in a shop or café, where you have to communicate with customers, or volunteering during a Duke of Edinburgh Award expedition, in which you have to talk and listen to your teammates.

Examples you could give of written communication include entering writing competitions, blogging and organising a petition for a cause that you're passionate about, and of course any essays you've written for school, especially if you have the grades or feedback to back it up.

Teamwork

The ability to get on and work with others is really important to employers.

This is an important employability skill because, unless you get a job where you're not expected to speak to a soul all day (unlikely!), it's pretty crucial that you can work well as part of a team.

Most jobs involve interacting with colleagues and you'll do well to prove

that you're confident in a group and that you enjoy working with others.

Practical examples you could put on your application to demonstrate this employability skill include playing in a sports team, joining an after-school club, or being part of a scheme like Young Enterprise, Scouts or Guides.

Initiative

Look at a selection of job adverts and you'll often come across something along the lines of "must be able to work independently and in a team".

While employers want to know that you can work well with your colleagues, they also like to see that you are motivated, proactive and can be trusted to use your own initiative – for example, by keeping your employability skills up-to-date with the latest developments in your area of work.

Show that initiative is one of your key skills by doing a free online course to learn a new skill, forming a new group or club or setting up your own business (e.g. washing cars in the neighbourhood after the local carwash closed).

Problem solving

Sadly, nothing in life is guaranteed to be plane sailing and your new boss will want to know that you're not going to run away screaming at the first sign of trouble.

Problem solving is among the most valuable employability skills in any job, and particularly in careers that deal with difficult or constantly changing situations.

Show that you're a top-notch problem solver with examples like competing in a maths challenge, being a member of the chess team, building a website or taking part in an orienteering event.

Computer skills

Most bosses will expect basic IT skills – and any coding you can add on top will be a bonus.

Most bosses will expect you to have basic IT (like Microsoft Office), making this is an essential addition to your list of employability skills.

For other jobs you will need to demonstrate that you have practical experience in more specific programmes – common ones include Photoshop, InDesign, content management systems like WordPress and working knowledge of HTML.

If you want to show off your IT and technical skills, make sure you give some good examples of where you've used them – for example, building your own website or app, or taking part in a coding or programming challenge.

Organisation

Being well-organised is an invaluable employability skill for most jobs and it's an absolute must for ones that involve working to a tight deadline, such as print and publishing.

Proving that time management is among your keys skills and showing that you can prioritise your workload will look really good on your CV. Examples of this include taking on a part-time job and managing your work and studies effectively, organising an event or editing the school newspaper.

Leadership

While it's important that you can work well as a team, being able to show you'd make a good leader or manager is an employability skill that will set you apart from many candidates.

Even if you're going in at an entry-level job that doesn't involve any line management responsibility at the moment, that could change in the future, particularly if you do well at work and impress the boss.

Examples that show off your ability to lead include being captain of a sports team, leader of a club or group, or volunteering as a team leader or mentor.

Hard work and dedication

It doesn't matter what job you do and in what industry – employers all want to know that you will work hard.

Show that you really do want to work for them (not just anyone) and that you care about, and take pride in, what you do, and you'll be pretty irresistible.

Practical examples to demonstrate these skills include taking after-school classes to improve your grades, studying an extra subject, volunteering, or doing a part-time job.

Creativity

Creativity is part of a new wave of employability skills

Creativity shows that you can think outside the box – a skill which, with the growth of innovative start ups and the huge world of opportunities that the Internet has opened up, is one of a new wave of essential employability skills.

Practical examples you could give of your creative skills include blogging, taking part in a school play or dance/music concert or talking about a photography or creative writing project you've done in your own time.

Numeracy

The ability to understand and work with numbers is important in virtually any job. We use maths every day to understand facts and figures, make decisions, and solve problems.

You don't just use your numeracy skills in maths and science. Subjects like art and design and IT are all about solving problems and making plans based on the information you have at your disposal.

Do you have a part-time job in a shop? Or get pocket money? If the answer's yes, you almost certainly use your numeracy skills to tot up the amounts, or put cash aside in your savings.

Reliability

Employers need people they can trust and rely on to run a great business. As well as being great at your job, your employers will want you to turn up on time, be there when you're needed, and do what's expected of you (and more!).

You could talk about your school/college attendance record, your commitment to any clubs or societies you're part of, or how your homework is always completed on time and to the highest standard.

⇨ The above information is reprinted with kind permission from Success At School. Please visit www.successatschool.org for further information.

Key facts

- 1.4 million adults were unemployed in the UK between August and October 2017 (the latest figure). (page 1)

- 4.3% of people aged 16 and over were unemployed from August to October 2017 – that's around one in every 23 people who want to work. This is down from 4.8% a year earlier and the lowest it has been since 1975. (page 1)

- 523,000 young people were unemployed from August to October 2017 (including 186,000 full-time students looking for part-time work). (page 1)

- The unemployment rate for 16- to 24-year-olds was 12%. This figure is lower than at the same time a year earlier (13%) and is the lowest it has been since 2004. (page 1)

- Those over 25 saw an increase of 4.3% in the minimum wage while under-25s saw 3.2%. (page 4)

- An estimated 2.1 million families will face an average loss of £1,600 a year, while 1.8 million will gain an average of £1,500. (page 6)

- A weekly total of £21.9 million in benefits goes unclaimed. (page 10)

- The gender pay gap for full-time employees in 2016 was 9.4%. (page 11)

- The gap for all employees (full-time and part-time) has reduced from 19.3% in 2015 to 18.1% in 2016. This gap is down from 27.5% in 1997. (page 11)

- The gender pay gap for part-time employees alone was minus 6.0% in 2016. This means female part-time employees earned 6.0% more than male part-time employees. (page 11)

- Almost nine in ten (87 per cent) of the UK's full-time workforce either currently work flexibly or would like to do so. (page 14)

- Seven in ten (73 per cent) of those aged 18 to 34 who are working full-time, doing so flexibly. (page 14)

- 72 per cent of those aged over 55 either currently work flexibly, would like to work flexibly or would prefer to work part-time. (page 14)

- In 2015, 85% of women between the ages of 25–49 without children were employed, exactly the same proportion as childless men employed in the same age group. (page 15)

- Only 16% of all women between the ages of 25–49 without dependent children worked part-time, while this proportion more than triples for women in the same age group with children to 52%. (page 15)

- At age 25, people on zero-hours contracts and those who were unemployed were less likely to report feeling healthy, compared to those in more secure employment. (page 17)

- Only 15% of people on zero-hours contracts want a new job compared to 5% of those in other contracts. (page 19)

- 53% of employees used one or more of work–life balance supports. (page 21)

- As many as 48% of people surveyed support higher tax and more public spending, up from 32% at the start of austerity in 2010. (page 26)

- Support for spending on benefits for disabled people is up to 67%, compared with 53% in 2010. (page 26)

- Since 2012, the Government has reported a steady decline in the number of 16–24-year-olds who spend time not in education, employment or training (NEET). (page 26)

- From January to March 2017, 800,000 (11.2%) young people were presently NEET – a 68,000 reduction on the same quarter in 2016. (page 26)

- Nearly two million young people between 16 and 24 spend some time NEET. (page 26)

- Young people in the UK are increasingly well-qualified – 79% to Level 2 or above, and nearly 40% to Level 3 or above. (page 27)

- For those with higher level qualifications (Level 3, Level 4 and above), whilst 10% are at risk of spending six months or more NEET, only 3% are at risk of being NEET for 12 months or longer. (page 27)

- Women are more likely to be economically inactive (66% of this group are female) while men are more likely to be unemployed (60% of this group are male). (page 27)

- The level of unemployment of 16–24-year-olds peaked in the UK during 2011, when it reached over 1 million (a rate of 22%) and continued to fall as the economy started to grow. By the end of 2014 youth unemployment fell to around 840,000 – at a rate of 18%. (page 29)

- 16–24-year-olds remain the highest group at risk of unemployment, with 35–49 year olds being the least at risk. (page 29)

- Youth unemployment in the EU as a whole stands at 21.4%. (page 29)

- There are 70,000 interns in the UK at any one time. (page 31)

- Roughly 10,000 graduates are carrying out an internship at six months post-graduation, with 20% of them doing so unpaid. (page 31)

- Almost 80% of young people were also offered a job at the end of their apprenticeship. (page 35)

- Those who progress on to study a Professional/Higher apprenticeship will increase earnings by an estimated £150,000 over a lifetime – with the bonus of no university debt. (page 36)

- 92% of apprentices feel their apprenticeship has positively improved their career prospects. (page 36)

- 56% of recent graduates felt that the biggest benefit of doing a degree was being 'more qualified' than others when applying for a job. (page 36)

Apprenticeship

A form of vocational training which involves learning a trade or skill through working. An apprentice will often shadow an experienced practitioner of a trade, learning the occupation 'on the job'. Some apprenticeships can take many years.

Entrepreneur

An individual who starts and runs their own business.

Equality Bill

The Equality Bill came into force from autumn 2010. The Bill sets out ground-breaking new laws which will help narrow the gap between rich and poor; require business to report on gender pay; outlaw age discrimination; and will significantly strengthen Britain's anti-discrimination legislation.

Flexible working

Any working pattern which allows an individual to vary the time or place in which work is done. Flexible working schemes include part-time work, flexitime and job sharing.

Internship

A placement in an organization, sometimes without pay, in order to gain work experience or satisfy requirements for a qualification.

Labour market

The market in which workers compete for jobs and employers compete for workers.

Minimum wage

The National Minimum Wage (NMW) is a minimum amount per hour that most workers in the UK are legally entitled to be paid. The level of NMW you are entitled to depends on your age.

National Insurance

Taxes paid by employees and employers.

National living wage

The national living wage is now £10.20 an hour for those living in London and £8.75 in the rest of the UK. This is the amount that the Government believes is the minimum people need to be paid in order to achieve a basic standard of living in which all necessities can be paid for.

NEET

Young people not in employment, education or training.

Pay gap

The gender pay gap refers to the difference between men and women's earnings. Currently, women earn on average 21% less than their male counterparts.

Pension

When someone reaches retirement age, they are entitled to receive a regular pension payment from the Government. This payment takes the place of a salary. Many people choose to pay into a private pension fund throughout their career, in order to save extra money for when they retire. Often, employers also pay into a pension fund for their employees. The State Pension Age is gradually increasing. The Pensions Act 2011 will see the State Pension Age for both men and women increase to 66 by October 2020 to "keep pace with increases in longevity (people living longer)".

Universal Credit

Universal Credit is the new benefit system in the UK. It replaces six means-tested benefits and tax credits: income-based Jobseeker's Allowance, Housing Benefit, Working Tax Credit, Child Tax Credit, income-based Employment and Support Allowance and Income Support.

Vocational

A qualification which is relevant to a particular career and can be expected to provide a route into that career.

Work–life balance

Having a measure of control over when, where and how you work, in order to enjoy an optimal quality of life. In a 2008 survey of Oxbridge graduates, a majority in every sector said they would prioritise work–life balance when thinking about their career.

Assignments

Brainstorming

⇨ With a partner, discuss what you know about unemployment in the UK. Draw a mind-map of all the things you think about in connection with the issue of unemployment.

⇨ In small groups, think about the different types of career paths people might follow after they leave school. List as many careers as you can think of, and include a note that explains whether each job requires a degree, A-levels, GCSEs, work experience, an apprenticeship, a college course, etc.

⇨ With a partner, discuss skills that employers may look for in employees. Design a diamond9 chart to rank the employability skills that are important.

⇨ In small groups, make a list of jobs that you associate with gender stereotyping and write them in two columns headed 'male' and 'female'. Rank the jobs from highest to lowest earnings in each column and discuss the groups' findings.

Research

⇨ Pick a career that interests you and research how you can achieve that career. Include training/routes into work and how much you are likely to earn.

⇨ Research the way in which the gender pay gap affects people. Write some notes on your findings and feedback to the rest of the class.

⇨ Choose a country in the EU and research their attitude to work and employment. Write some notes on your findings and feedback to your class.

⇨ Research the opportunities afforded by self-employment, and some careers where being self-employed is an option. Write some notes and feedback to your class.

⇨ In small groups, create a questionnaire about future employment. Ask the rest of your class to complete the questionnaire and feedback to your class the results.

Design

⇨ Using the article "Why zero-hours contracts are becoming increasingly popular" and "Being on a zero-hours contract is bad for your heath", create a leaflet that explains the positives and negatives of zero-hours contracts.

⇨ Design a poster that will encourage people who are unemployed and not currently seeking work, to look for employment.

⇨ Design a poster to persuade people to either go to university or become an apprentice. You can use the article "Apprenticeships vs university" to help you.

⇨ Design an app that would help people improve their work–life balance. Use the article "Taking control of your work–life balance" for ideas.

Oral

⇨ Think about a job you would like to do in the future and create a five-minute presentation that explores the qualifications and experience you might need in order to enter that profession.

⇨ Discuss with a partner, what work means to you and how it could improve your personal well-being.

⇨ Role-play with a partner an interview for a job in an office. Discuss and make notes afterwards on the positive and negative things that each of you said.

⇨ Discuss with someone who is currently employed about their work. Ask them things such as "How did you get into work?", "What qualifications did you need?", "Have you changed career?" Think of your own questions and make notes on their answers.

Reading/writing

⇨ Read the article "The national minimum wage and living wage rates". Calculate how much money a 20-year-old would make, per week, if they worked 40 hours and were paid the National Minimum Wage. Now, do the same for a 27-year-old, if they worked 35 hours per week. Create a budget detailing what you would spend on rent, food, bills and leisure expenses.

⇨ Read the article "Yes, you're (still) better off working than on benefit" and write a summary of why you would be better off financially, being in employment.

⇨ Read the article "How young people can solve the youth unemployment crisis" then think of an idea for a business. Write an outline for a business plan which details your business idea, your start-up costs and why you think it will be successful.

⇨ Imagine that you are a parent who wishes to return to work after having a baby. Write a letter to your employer requesting flexible working. Include in the letter why you think that they should allow you to do this.

⇨ Write a paragraph on where you think you will be in ten-years time. Include a bullet-point list on how you think you will achieve your goals.

⇨ Watch the film *The Intern* or *The Internship*, and write notes on why you think that someone would take part in an internship. Do you think that they are suitable for someone who is looking for work experience, or for someone who is changing career?

Index

Acknowledgements

The publisher is grateful for permission to reproduce the material in this book. While every care has been taken to trace and acknowledge copyright, the publisher tenders its apology for any accidental infringement or where copyright has proved untraceable. The publisher would be pleased to come to a suitable arrangement in any such case with the rightful owner.

Images

All images courtesy of iStock except pages 4, 12, 19, 21 and 38: Unsplash, and pages 10, 13, 22, 23, 35 and 36: Pixabay

Illustrations

Don Hatcher: pages 17 & 34. Simon Kneebone: pages 3 & 20. Angelo Madrid: pages 9 & 30.

Additional acknowledgements

With thanks to the Independence team: Shelley Baldry, Danielle Lobban, Jackie Staines and Jan Sunderland.

Tina Brand

Cambridge, June 2018